healthy eating for
lower cholesterol

Daniel Green with

Catherine Collins RD

healthy eating for
lower
cholesterol

Photography by Lis Parsons

Kyle Cathie Ltd

contents

dedication

To my daughter, Eleanor (Daniel Green)

For Allan, Sophie, Alex and the Blackmores (Catherine Collins)

important note

The information and advice contained in this book are intended as a general guide to
healthy eating and are not specific to individuals or their particular circumstances. This
book is not intended to replace treatment by a qualified practitioner. Neither the authors
nor the publishers can be held responsible for claims arising from the inappropriate use of
any dietary regime. Do not attempt self-diagnosis or self-treatment for serious or long-
term conditions without consulting a medical professional or qualified practitioner.

foreword by H·E·A·R·T UK

High cholesterol is directly associated with cardiovascular disease, and new national guidelines for healthy cholesterol levels, recently revised to be more stringent, mean that a great many of us need to bring our cholesterol down. Whilst our doctors fill out hundreds of prescriptions for cholesterol-lowering drugs, healthy nutritional eating remains a proven and supremely effective way of managing our cholesterol levels in a natural way, and is surely the best place to start.

Today, we are presented with so much good lifestyle advice it can often be difficult to know what is essential or relevant to us personally. We are always moving on to the next lifestyle trend with little regard for the sound, long standing advice that, if we look properly, continues to stand us in good stead. However, this new publication is an example of the very best kind of advice; a book that you can keep coming back to in order to achieve both the best quality in cooking terms and discover what's best for your heart and soul.

Healthy Eating for Lower Cholesterol provides a thoroughly reliable source of medically approved health advice that is the best line of defence against cardio-vascular disease that can affect us and our families in so many serious and unexpected ways. At H·E·A·R·T UK we specialise in the treatment of the genetic disorder Familial Hypercholesterolaemia or FH for short. This affects around 120,000 people in the UK population, who unless diagnosed are likely to suffer premature heart attacks and strokes in their thirties and forties. Even men in their twenties can die from a first attack, and although these tragic events can be prevented with correct diagnosis, treatment and lifestyle management, 100,000 people remain unaware of their inherited condition.

This book is therefore a must-read, as it helps us to understand the basics of cardio-vascular disease, how and why it develops, the essential role of cholesterol in the disease process, how the 'bad' type of cholesterol differs from the 'good' and how we can manage to keep it and other risk factors under control.

I am delighted to champion *Healthy Eating for Lower Cholesterol*. I highly recommend it as a practical, healthy eating guide for the whole family that represents an investment in the future but requires no sacrifice at all… bon appetit.

Michael Livingston
Director – H·E·A·R·T UK

introduction

Few of us ever pause to consider our heart and circulation, despite the crucial part that they play in enabling us to lead a full and active life. Often, it is only when we're running for a train or exercising at the gym that we become aware of just how hard our circulation is working to keep up with the extra demands imposed on it.

Statistics show that cardiovascular disease ('cardio' – heart; 'vascular' – blood vessel) remains the UK's biggest killer, claiming the life of one in five men, and one in six women; and nearly half of all deaths in Britain from coronary heart disease are due to high blood cholesterol levels. Background damage to blood vessels has already begun by the time we approach our late twenties (even though it may be another fifteen years or so before symptoms declare themselves), but by taking steps to change our diet and lifestyle we can greatly influence the health of our heart and circulation.

Time for a change

The fact that you've picked up this book indicates that you may be interested in – or perhaps concerned about – your heart health, and the risk of circulatory disease. Perhaps a health check has shown a raised cholesterol level? Or you have had a wake-up call from seeing a friend or relative suffer a stroke or heart attack and the way in which it has affected their quality of life. Or you may simply have decided that it's time to address what goes on inside your body in order to maintain your current good health well into old age.

Whatever the reason for your interest, the information in *Healthy Eating for Lower Cholesterol* will help you to choose a healthier way of eating, and you will be amazed at the abundance of foods allowed. It's a very positive diet, which, together with Dan's recipes, will give you all the inspiration you need.

The cholesterol conundrum

Of all the substances that our body produces, cholesterol seems to hold the record for bad press. Yet, what people often tend to overlook is that cholesterol is essential for human life – so important, in fact, that the body makes its own supply so that it does not have to rely on dietary intake.

What exactly is cholesterol?

Cholesterol forms the basis of steroid hormones such as testosterone and progesterone (sex hormones), cortisol (for stress adaptation), and vitamin D (for healthy bones). It also helps to build and maintain healthy cell membranes, and the insulating sheath around nerve fibres which act like 'broadband', speeding nerve signals to and from the brain. Also, the liver uses cholesterol to make bile salts that help to digest food more effectively.

The majority of the cholesterol in our circulation is made by the liver from dietary saturated fat. The remainder comes from food containing cholesterol, such as fatty meat, eggs, dairy foods, seafood, fish and poultry. The liver ultimately controls blood cholesterol levels, reducing its cholesterol production when cholesterol from the diet is available.

the cholesterol couriers

Cholesterol has to travel from the liver to wherever it is needed in the body, so transport via the circulation is inevitable. Cholesterol is too 'waxy' to dissolve in blood, so it is transported around the body in a number of tiny 'couriers', called lipoproteins. A blood cholesterol level reflects the amount of cholesterol transported by these lipoprotein couriers at the time of a blood test. In general, a high blood cholesterol level increases your risk of cardiovascular disease. However, some couriers are considered 'safer' than others, so the goal of cholesterol management is to lower the levels of unsafe couriers, whilst maintaining more stable forms of cholesterol transport.

Just as vehicles on the road vary in size, so do our cholesterol couriers. Unlike road traffic, however, each lipoprotein can be remodelled by the liver into another type, changing its composition in the process. So, whilst they may start out as very large, buoyant and rich in fat, they gradually shrink in size, becoming smaller, denser cholesterol couriers, carrying less fat.

LDL ('bad' cholesterol)

Low-density lipoprotein (LDL) is the main cholesterol courier in our circulation; it transports cholesterol and triglycerides (fats) from cells that produce more than they can use to cells and tissues in need. Around 70 per cent of our circulating cholesterol is carried by LDL couriers. They vary in size depending on their triglyceride and cholesterol content – in healthy individuals LDL carriers are large and relatively few in number; in contrast small, dense LDL carriers are strongly associated with heart and circulatory disease, possibly because their small size allows them to penetrate the artery walls. LDL cholesterol is often termed 'bad' cholesterol for this reason, but its level can be reduced by diet and lifestyle changes.

Other cholesterol couriers

In addition to LDL, there are other cholesterol transport couriers. Chylomicron couriers transport cholesterol and dietary fat from the digestive tract to the liver, and then very low-density lipoproteins (VLDLs) haul triglycerides around the body for delivery to our body cells, before returning to the liver for reprocessing into LDL couriers. VLDL couriers may be likened to manufacturers' lorries, delivering large quantities of goods (triglycerides) to a central warehouse for distribution by the LDL couriers. Triglycerides are an independent risk factor for cardiovascular disease, often raised in people who are overweight, drink too much alcohol, or have Type 2 diabetes (see page 19). Controlling blood sugar, reducing alcohol intake, and increasing physical activity all independently reduce the blood triglyceride level.

HDL ('good' cholesterol)

The smallest lipoprotein, high-density lipoprotein (HDL), is made in the liver from the remains of LDL cholesterol. Unlike other cholesterol couriers, HDL offers a 'collection' rather than 'delivery' service, collecting surplus cholesterol and fat from cells, and returning them to the liver for processing and removal. HDL also has the ability to 'pull' cholesterol and fat from newly formed deposits on the artery walls, helping to maintain healthy arteries.

Once excess cholesterol has been returned to the liver, it can be converted into bile acids for transfer to the gallbladder, or it can be recycled into lipoprotein couriers again. Each day the liver produces up to 2g of cholesterol and 0.4g of bile salts, the latter to replenish losses from the bile salt pool. Reducing the recycling of bile salts is how cholesterol-lowering stanol and sterol esters (see page 34) and soluble fibre function (see page 24).

How can I check my cholesterol levels?

The only way to establish your exact cholesterol profile is by having a blood test – often called a lipid profile. Lipid is a collective term for fats in the blood, and a blood test can tell you how much cholesterol is present, and what type. A random blood test can measure total and HDL cholesterol levels. A fasting blood test (where you fast for at least 12 hours beforehand, drinking nothing but water) can measure LDL cholesterol and triglyceride levels in addition, giving a more comprehensive result.

Ideal cholesterol levels

The goal of cholesterol management is to reduce the risk of cardiovascular disease. To put this into context, a high cholesterol level alone is thought to be responsible for 46 per cent of all premature deaths from coronary heart disease in the UK. Population studies may suggest a ballpark value for cholesterol levels, but our own individual cholesterol level and risk of cardiovascular disease are tempered by our lifestyle and other health concerns, such as high blood pressure. The table below gives guideline levels for each of the cholesterol couriers for general health, but the more stringent goals (the 'optimal' levels) have been devised by the six leading societies dealing with cardiovascular disease in the UK. Both sets of values are relevant for the general population. If you also have diabetes, high blood pressure or rheumatoid arthritis, then the optimal rather than guideline values should be your goal.

How is cholesterol measured?

Cholesterol is measured in 'mmols', a measurement of cholesterol concentration in each litre of blood (mmol/ L). This is a world standard unit for measuring cholesterol except in the USA, where the preferred measurement is the weight of cholesterol in each 100ml of blood (mg/dL). Ideal blood cholesterol levels are quoted in both measurements (see table).

A simple way to remember the desirable level of cholesterol couriers is that HDL should be High, LDL should be Low, and VLDL (akin to triglyceride level) should be Very Low!

Guideline cholesterol levels
Total cholesterol: 5 mmol/L
  (195mg/dL), or less
LDL cholesterol: 3 mmol/L
  (115mg/dL), or less
Triglycerides: 1.5 mmol/L
  (57mg/dL) or less
HDL cholesterol: above 0.9mmol/L
  (35mg/dL)

Optimal levels
Total cholesterol: 4 mmol/L
  (156mg/dL), or less
LDL cholesterol: 2 mmol/L
  (77mg/dL), or less
HDL cholesterol: above 1.5 mmol/L
  (58mg/dL)

the artery highways

In order for the couriers to deliver their loads effectively and safely, they need a healthy transport system to travel by – i.e. the arteries, veins and capillaries. Research suggests that we should not consider our total and LDL cholesterol levels in isolation but also how well our arteries are maintained. The health of our artery highways and their ability to resist damage are the focus of most new research into cardiovascular disease.

Our body works hard to keep our artery surfaces fully repaired and so less prone to damage. Arteries are made of three layers. A strong outer 'coat' surrounds a middle layer of muscles that allow the artery to widen or contract as needed to control our blood pressure. An inner layer of smooth, flat cells (called the 'endothelium') creates the 'non-stick' inner lining of the artery which makes for smooth blood flow. The endothelium protects the artery, repelling toxic substances and marshalling defences if the blood vessel becomes inflamed or damaged. 'Resurfacing' of damaged endothelium is achieved by the components of a healthy diet (see pages 20–33).

How a cholesterol plaque is formed

In much the same way that a lorry will sometimes hit a pothole in a road, causing it to shed some of its load, naturally occurring damage to the smooth endothelium surface can encourage

circulating LDL to deposit cholesterol. This can burrow below the endothelium layer, settling onto the muscular middle layer of the artery. Less stable LDL couriers (for example, those carrying 'oxidised' cholesterol), are more likely to deposit their unstable cholesterol load.

At this early stage, HDL couriers travelling along the artery may notice the cholesterol deposit, and can collect it from the artery wall for return to the liver, thus preventing development of an atheroma (or plaque). If it is not collected, however, the deposit generates local inflammation within the artery wall, attracting the interest of passing white blood cells. These then enter the breach and successfully attack the cholesterol, but in so doing become entrapped beneath the artery surface, forming a foam-like deposit trapped inside the artery wall.

Finally, in a damage-limitation exercise the endothelium surface forms a protective fibrin cap, resealing the surface and entombing the cholesterol, white blood cells and other debris (collectively known as an atheroma, or plaque) within the blood vessel wall. Remodelling of the fibrin 'cap' over the plaque eventually leads to a scar resistant to the natural 'stretch' of the artery wall. This hardening effect on the arteries is called athero-sclerosis.

Over time, the atheroma increases in size. Initially it is accommodated by an outward bulge in the artery wall (called an 'aneurysm'). Eventually, the strong

outer coat of the artery resists any further bulge, and the atheroma begins to push inwards, often rupturing the fibrin cap formed long ago to contain it. This has two possible outcomes. Either the rupture will attract red blood cells to form another clot to reseal, which can be dislodged into the circulation, eventually blocking a smaller blood vessel 'downstream'; or the ruptured plaque may shower atheroma debris into the circulation, with the same devastating outcome.

These are the principal mechanisms of a catastrophic heart attack or stroke occurring without warning, often resulting in major disability or death. Using ultrasound, it has been shown, fright-eningly, that unstable plaque can rupture when as little as 20 per cent of a blood vessel is obstructed by an atheroma.

The effects on health of atherosclerosis

As well as cardiovascular catastrophies there are chronic symptoms associated with atherosclerosis, or hardening of the arteries, and these can compromise quality of life.

Angina is a pain across the chest, and sometimes the arms, shoulders or jaw, brought on by exercise. The extra demands made on the heart by exercise increase its need for oxygen, but 'furred' arteries have lost their ability to dilate, preventing the demands for additional blood to the heart muscle from being met. The resulting pain is the heart sustaining something similar to a 'stitch in the side', and relief is experienced only when exercise is stopped and the heart has restored its oxygen demands.

Peripheral vascular disease (PVD) is the obstruction (by atherosclerosis) of the large leg arteries. Failure to meet the metabolic demands of the legs and feet during walking can cause severe pain (termed intermittent claudication), hampering mobility.

Transient ischaemic attack (TIA) is often referred to as a 'mini-stroke' and is usually caused by a small blood clot blocking an artery in the brain, resulting in a temporary disturbance of blood supply and a brief lapse in mental function, generally lasting for less than 24 hours before recovery is made. TIAs are a warning of the potential for a more devastating stroke, so are treated seriously by doctors.

The cholesterol–circulation link

Since as far back as the 1950s it has been known that raised blood cholesterol – particularly LDL cholesterol – increases your risk of heart and circulatory disease. But until recently it has been unclear as to exactly why cardiovascular disease can occur in people with normal cholesterol levels.

That each developing plaque represents a tiny pocket of inflammation within the artery wall has helped researchers to prove that any inflammation in the body – obvious or not – will affect how robust the artery will be in terms of resisting damage.

Inflammation is now considered a major cause of damage to the endothelium surface, priming an inflammatory process that accelerates the rate of cholesterol deposition and, by extension, atherosclerosis. It has been shown that people with rheumatoid arthritis – a severe inflammatory condition – have twice the risk of death from cardiovascular disease when compared with the general population. Reducing inflammation within the body is, therefore, a prime target for cholesterol control.

reducing your risk factors

Medical research has helped to determine risk factors that identify those at high risk of cardiovascular disease. There are some factors that you can't change, including advancing age or a genetic predisposition; most, however, can be modified by changes in your diet or lifestyle. In addition to a raised blood cholesterol, the following are all major causes of premature death from cardiovascular disease:

* lack of physical activity
* smoking
* obesity
* high blood pressure

And the more risk factors you have, the higher your risk of coronary heart disease.

Physical activity

Our modern lifestyle does little to encourage regular exercise, and many of us take no physical activity during a typical week. Individuals recording less than half an hour's physical activity a week are almost three times more likely to die in the short term than those who are more active.

Regular activity has proven positive health benefits, particularly for heart health. A single exercise session can beneficially reduce triglyceride levels by an average of 20 per cent and raise HDL cholesterol by 10 per cent. Regular exercise leads to favourable changes in blood pressure, blood lipids, blood glucose, insulin and clotting factors. It also reduces the risk of circulatory disease, and slows the enlargement of any existing atheroma. What's more, the calories expended during regular exercise help with weight management, and increasing muscle tone improves blood sugar and cholesterol levels.

Fortunately, gym membership isn't required for this benefit! Thirty minutes a day of regular activity such as brisk walking, gardening, cycling, or dancing are all beneficial for heart health, but any exercise is proven to be better than none. You should walk or exercise enough to leave you feeling warm and slightly out of breath. If you are unused to physical

	Factors that increase cholesterol levels	Factors that increase inflammation levels
Factors you can't change	* Increasing age and in particular being over 45 * Being male * Genetic predisposition to heart disease	* High blood levels of inflammatory blood proteins: homocysteine and C-reactive protein (CRP) * Background inflammatory states, e.g. arthritis
Factors you can change	* Inactivity and a lack of exercise * Smoking * Obesity/being overweight * High saturated fat intake * High intake of trans fats * Excess alcohol intake * Uncontrolled stress and anger	* Smoking * Obesity/being overweight * High saturated fat intake * High intake of trans fats * High intake of plant-based polyunsaturates (omega-6) * Poorly controlled diabetes * High blood pressure * Low or absent intake of omega-3 polyunsaturates * Lack of anti-oxidant nutrients * Excess alcohol intake * Excessive iron intake

exertion, gradually build it up over several weeks. Research suggests you need around 60 minutes of exercise each day if you want to lose weight.

Smoking

Smoking is a major cause of heart disease, other circulatory diseases and cancer, and there is no 'safe' level of usage. Smoking a pack of cigarettes a day doubles the risk of a heart attack.

The effects of smoking are three-fold. Nicotine constricts arteries, reducing blood supply to the heart and other tissues. Carbon monoxide from inhaled smoke reduces the amount of oxygen that can be carried in the bloodstream, and the combination of reduced oxygen delivery from reduced blood supply can damage the heart and other tissues. Nicotine and free radicals released from inhaled smoke damage the endothelium, initiating and accelerating atherosclerosis. Smoking also increases the levels of blood-clotting proteins, increases blood pressure and lowers levels of 'good' HDL cholesterol – a combination that is damaging to the heart and other tissues. To continue smoking removes any health benefits possible from other advice in this book. Take advantage of 'stop smoking' campaigns to save your health.

Obesity

Obesity is an increasing health risk in the Western world. Most adults are overweight, and obesity impacts significantly on good health. Obesity is associated with an increased risk of diabetes and hypertension (high blood pressure), which alone and together are associated with an accelerated rate of atherosclerosis.

Body fat is not inert, but generates biologically active substances (called adipokines) capable of increasing background inflammation, and accelerating atherosclerosis. Healthy people with a higher body weight have higher blood levels of protein markers of inflammation (such as C-reactive protein, or CRP), and a three-fold increased risk of heart disease – and this is the case whether or not blood cholesterol levels are raised.

Losing just 10 per cent of your body weight if you are overweight carries significant health benefits, reducing the release of adipokines from the diminished body fat stores. Crash dieting is not the answer, but following a healthy diet with modest calorie restriction (between 1400 and 1800 kcal a day) will result in weight loss. Every 0.5kg of fat contains the equivalent of 3500 kcal, so reducing calorie intake to 500 kcal a day below your body's energy needs (see box) will help you to lose 0.5kg of fat per week.

Apple or pear?
The area in which your body stores its excess fat can influence health risks. A 'pear' shape (in which excess fat is stored around the hips and thighs) carries a lower cardiovascular risk than an 'apple' shape (in which body fat is stored around the waist). 'Apples' have higher levels of background inflammation, easily measured using blood protein markers. They also are more likely to have insulin resistance (increasing the likelihood of diabetes), in tandem with a high blood pressure, cholesterol and triglycerides. A combination of obesity, insulin resistance and other factors is referred to as the 'metabolic syndrome'.

Waist measurements rather than weight alone more accurately identify whether people are at risk of heart disease. Test yourself by comparing your waist size with the guide on the following page, and measuring your waist midway distant from the lower rib and the hip bone. Your tape measure should cross the belly button, not swing low 'below the bulge' as your trouser waistband might.

Average energy needs of adults (UK recommendations)
(taken from COMA Report, Dietary Reference Values, 1991)

Age	Men: kcal per day	Women: kcal per day
19–50 years	2550	1940
50–64 years	2380	1900
65–74 years	2330	1900
75+ years	2100	1810

Waist measurements

	Ideal value	Increased risk – should not increase weight further	Substantial risk – should actively try to lose weight
Women	80cm or less	80cm or more	88cm or more
Men	94cm or less	94cm or more	102cm or more

Waist-to-hip ratio (WHR)

This ratio appears to be a more beneficial guide in identifying people at risk of cardiovascular disease across all weight ranges. Measure the widest part of your hips, then divide your waist measurement by your hip measurement. For example, if your waist is 80cm, and your hip size is 96cm, your WHR = 80÷96 = 0.83. An ideal value is 0.83 for women, and 0.90 for men. Any waist-to-hip ratio above these values is a strong predictor for cardiovascular disease.

Clothing sizes

Recent research in nutrition has shown that, in the absence of weighing scales or a tape measure, clothing sizes can be a useful marker for risk of cardiovascular disease. For men, a trouser waist size greater than 38 inches in UK/US sizing, or 97cm in European sizing, predicts a greatly increased risk of heart disease, high blood pressure and diabetes. For women, a size 18 or above (size 16 in the USA or 48 in Europe) carries similar health risks.

Diet

The main influence on cholesterol levels from our diet is the amount and type of fat that we consume (see pages 26–32), but other factors also play a part. A regular, modest alcohol intake appears to have some cardioprotective benefits, helping your liver to form more of the

beneficial HDL cholesterol. A high alcohol intake, however, will remove any such benefits because of its toxic effects on the liver. (See also page 32.)

Following the dietary advice in the next section will naturally increase your intake of dietary antioxidant nutrients to help protect your body against free-radical damage.

Stress

In moderation, mental and physical stress appear to be beneficial to the body. However, sustained high levels of stress injures blood vessels, promotes athero-sclerosis, and increases circulating levels of the blood-clotting protein fibrinogen, more than doubling your risk of cardio-

vascular disease. The stress hormones cortisol and adrenalin are behind these changes. A person with an angry, hostile personality has a significantly increased risk of cardiovascular disease. Speak to your GP if you think stress is affecting your mental or physical health – there are many programmes available for you to learn techniques to help manage your stress.

Diabetes

Diabetes is on the increase in the Western world, and it is estimated that for every person diagnosed with the condition, another remains undiagnosed. Type I diabetes occurs when the body switches off insulin production. This type requires life-long control of blood sugar levels by injection of insulin. The most common type of diabetes in the UK is Type 2 diabetes, caused not by a lack of insulin, but by insulin resistance. In Type 2 diabetes, the body produces

insulin, but its effect in clearing excessive blood sugar levels is compromised by 'resistance' of body cells to accept it. Type 2 diabetes is linked to obesity, particularly central obesity with extra weight around the waist. Losing weight improves insulin usage and blood sugar levels, and also reduces the increased risk of cardiovascular disease.

High blood pressure

Blood pressure is the force of blood pushing against the artery walls, and it is necessary to ensure that blood supply can reach every cell in the body.

A blood pressure reading comprises two numbers, one appearing above the other: e.g., 120/80 (an ideal reading). The higher figure (120 in this case) is the systolic pressure, representing the surge in pressure generated with every heartbeat. The lower figure (80) represents the diastolic pressure – the background

pressure of blood between heartbeats.

Blood pressure varies throughout the day, being lowest when you sleep and rising when you get up, or when you are exercising, nervous, or stressed. Transient rises in blood pressure are the body's way of adapting to its environment and are perfectly normal. However, if your blood pressure constantly measures 140/90 or higher, you have high blood pressure (also called hypertension). Left unmanaged, hypertension can cause the heart to enlarge as it needs to work harder. It can also accelerate damage to the arteries, facilitating the process of atherosclerosis (see page 14) and increasing the risk of cardiovascular disease and kidney damage.

High blood pressure should not be ignored, and can be controlled with a healthy diet, adopting the Mediterranean style of eating (see page 20) in tandem with reduced salt and alcohol intake. If you are overweight, losing 10 per cent of your body weight will help to lower blood pressure. Increasing physical activity levels and, if necessary, medication can also help to control the condition.

In a nutshell

So, to summarise, maintaining a healthy heart and circulation requires a two-pronged approach: control of cholesterol has a significant effect on health and, at the same time, addressing health, diet and lifestyle issues can help to reduce inflammation within the body, protecting the artery walls from damage.

Blood pressure readings

Classification	Systolic blood pressure (mmHg)*	Diastolic blood pressure (mmHg)
Ideal	Less than 120	Less than 80
Normal	Less than 130	Less than 85
High normal (pre-hypertensive)	131-139	85-89
Hypertension	140 or above	90 or above

*mmHg = millimetres of mercury

the heart-healthy diet

In the 1960s an ambitious medical trial was devised to compare diet, lifestyle and ongoing heart disease rates across seven countries, selected at the time for their recognised differences in heart disease rates. Led by Dr Ancel Keys, an eminent American physiologist, the results proved revolutionary, demonstrating a five- to tenfold difference in the rates of heart disease between populations.

The 'Seven Countries Study', as it became known, provided evidence that a diet abundant in vegetables, fruit, pasta, bread and olive oil, and sparing with meat, eggs, butter and full-fat dairy products, reduced the occurrence of heart disease. It also highlighted the type rather than the amount of dietary fat influenced this effect. A higher intake of olive oil and omega-3 polyunsaturates from oily fish appeared to reduce the risk of heart disease and cancer. The population of Crete had the lowest rate of death from heart disease, and the longest life expectancy of all the countries studied, hence this healthful diet became known simply as the 'Mediterranean diet'.

Of course, there is not just one Mediterranean diet, since the countries surrounding the Mediterranean – from Africa to Europe – incorporate many cultural and food differences. Yet despite this, there are also many similarities, including an emphasis on plant-based foods (vegetables, fruit, legumes and wholegrains), along with a relatively low consumption of meat, a moderate intake of low-fat dairy products, modest alcohol intake, and a relatively high intake of olive oil.

Key aspects of the cardioprotective Mediterranean diet

✳ Abundance of vegetables, salads and fruit, rich in cardioprotective nutrients

✳ High in monounsaturated fats, such as extra virgin olive oil

✳ Balanced omega-3/omega-6 polyunsaturated fat ratio

✳ Emphasis on wholegrain breads and cereals, and legumes

✳ Moderate amounts of lean meat, fish, dairy foods and eggs

✳ Only a small amount of alcohol

There are two key nutritional approaches to reducing cardiovascular disease and maintaining good health. First, controlling the level and type of circulating cholesterol will minimise the risk of LDL cholesterol offloading into the artery wall. Second, reducing background inflammation in the body reduces the sensitivity of the endothelium, improving its ability to defend the artery against attack from blood cholesterol, blood sugar, or high blood pressure.

The Mediterranean diet deftly addresses both of these concerns, as well as aiding in the prevention and improved management of other chronic diseases such as high blood pressure and diabetes and cancer. Recent research strongly suggests additional benefits in preventing other diseases of ageing such as cancer, dementia and Alzheimers disease.

Being a whole diet, as opposed to so many others that concentrate on a specific factor, such as fat intake, for example, the Mediterranean diet has the edge for a number of reasons:
✳ The wide variety of foods makes it easy to follow – for lifelong benefit
✳ The high antioxidant content of the diet (being abundant in vegetables, fruit, and extra virgin olive oil) reduces heart disease and cancer risk, and can improve the symptoms and management of other chronic diseases
✳ It is a style of eating that can be adapted to different populations, tailored to local foods, but always maintaining the same health benefits. Many Asian countries, for example, have diets with a similar profile (sometimes termed MediterrAsian!) and also enjoy low rates of cardiovascular disease.

The next section expands on what makes a diet 'Mediterranean', and explains how certain foods can complement each other to enhance the health benefits. The closer you can make your diet to the Mediterranean model, the better your cholesterol control will be and, with it, the likelihood of healthy arteries.

Fruit and vegetables in the cardioprotective diet

'Eat more fruit and vegetables' is the simple yet profound health message that forms the cornerstone of the Mediterranean

diet. A high vegetable and fruit intake is common in healthy populations enjoying a low incidence of heart disease, stroke and cancer. Vegetables and fruit are nature's own 'functional foods', so powerful that the World Health Organisation recommends a daily intake of at least 400g a day – loosely translated as the 'five a day' with which most of us are now familiar. Fresh, frozen, tinned and dried fruits and vegetables and their juices all 'count' towards the daily five. Despite this, however, few of us manage even a scant three portions a day.

Nature's functional foods

Fruit and vegetables provide us with a host of plant substances that are essential for health. Phytochemicals (see right) and dietary fibres enhance their natural 'functionality' and their low calorie content offsets the calorie-rich Western diet that

contributes to obesity. The average Mediterranean diet provides around 125 kcal per 100g of food eaten, compared with 160 kcal per 100g in the typical Western diet. Adopting this way of eating is a sure way to eat a lot more and weigh a lot less.

The antioxidants present in fruit and vegetables include vitamins, minerals and phytochemicals (plant chemicals). Vitamin C, beta carotene, vitamin E, zinc and selenium protect the body from damaging 'free radicals', natural by-products of oxygen metabolism within cells. Free radicals can be harnessed for useful purposes but a surplus can cause cell and tissue injury. Certain lifestyle aspects, such as smoking and excessive sun exposure, are also known to trigger excessive free-radical production.

Vitamins and minerals
Fruit and vegetables provide an abundance of vitamins and minerals

– tiny nutrients essential for life and which support and protect the body in a myriad of ways. The B group vitamins, for example, help to release energy in the cells, protect against anaemia, and to maintain a healthy skin and nerve supply. Folic acid – a B vitamin found naturally in green leafy vegetables, oranges and pulses – works with vitamins B6 and B12 to reduce blood levels of homocysteine (a toxic by-product of protein metabolism known to cause damage to the endothelium and increase the risk of heart disease and stroke).

Phytochemicals
Plants contain hundreds of non-nutrient substances called 'phytochemicals' that provide the wide range of colours and flavours present in fruit and vegetables. Each plant colour supplies a different class of phytochemical, so it is important to ensure that your diet includes an assortment of colours in order to enhance the usefulness of the fruit and

What counts as a five-a-day portion?

The servings below should give you an idea of what comprises a 'portion':
1 apple, pear or banana
1 handful of grapes, strawberries or cherries
2 tomatoes, plums or satsumas
1 large slice of melon
150ml fruit juice
1 tablespoon dried fruit/3 dried apricots
1 dessert bowl mixed salad
2 tablespoons cooked vegetables

Notes: Potatoes do not 'count' as a portion and each item can 'count' only once, irrespective of the amount eaten – it is the blend of colours and flavours that gives synergism to the plant-chemical benefits (so eating two or more apples, for example, is therefore just more of the same). (See also Phytochemicals above.)

vegetables you are eating. The UK Stroke Association's prevention campaign 'Eat a Rainbow' highlights this approach.

The importance of phytochemicals in providing additional health benefits beyond those of vitamin and mineral intake is increasingly recognised. Many possess powerful antioxidant abilities which are far greater than the effects of established antioxidant nutrients such as vitamin C. For example, lutein helps to protect the eye retina from UV light damage and lycopene protects against prostate cancer. Beta-carotene (derived from foods, not from high-dose supplements) seems to have protective properties against cancer in tandem with vitamin C and E intake.

Flavonoids such as quercetin enhance vitamin C function, and catechins (found in tea) provide a substantial antioxidant load. Cocoa flavonoids have cardiovascular benefit, reducing LDL cholesterol, blood stickiness and background inflammation. So two squares of dark chocolate daily with a minimum 70 per cent cocoa solid content provide a substantial flavonoid load without excessive calorie or fat intake. The range of colours in extra virgin olive oil reflects its polyphenol content, providing antioxidant benefits. The deeper the colour (green or yellow), the higher the polyphenol content. Paler coloured, refined olive oils lack the polyphenol content.

Nuts

Frequent nut consumption appears to offer some protection against heart disease. Diets supplemented with nuts, particularly almonds, macadamia nuts and walnuts, show a beneficial reduction in LDL cholesterol and total cholesterol, and a significant reduction in coronary heart disease risk. Regular nut and seed consumption (around 140g per week) reduces blood levels of inflammatory factors, indicating that nuts and seeds can help protect against arterial damage. Nuts also provide protein, magnesium, potassium, copper, vitamin E, folic acid, fibre and the essential fatty acid alpha-

Where to find your phytochemicals

Antioxidant phytochemicals:	Found in:
Lutein (carotenoid)	Corn, spinach, kale, E161b food colouring
Lycopene (carotenoid)	Tomatoes, watermelons, pink grapefruit, papayas, rosehips
Beta-carotene	Carrots, tomatoes, peppers, pumpkins
Anthocyanins	Aubergines, cherries, red grapes, blackberries, blackcurrants, bilberries, red cabbages, E163 food colouring
Quercetin	Citrus fruits, green and black tea, onions, apples, broccoli
Catechins	Tea, chocolate, apples

Fat and calorie content of nuts and seeds*

Nuts	g fat per 100g	Kcal per 100g
Chestnuts	3g	170 kcal
Sunflower seeds	48g	581 kcal
Peanuts	50g	589 kcal
Cashews	48g	573 kcal
Pistachios	55g	601 kcal
Almonds	57g	621 kcal
Sesame seeds	58g	598 kcal
Brazil nuts	68g	682 kcal
Walnuts	69g	688 kcal

*All values given are for an edible portion, not including shells.

Five ways to 'five-a-day'*

1 Enjoy a glass or 200ml carton of fruit juice every day, or try a mini 'health' drink (shot-size vegetable drinks or fruit smoothies).
2 Always have a piece of fruit with your lunch and choose fresh or dried fruit for a healthy between-meal snack.
3 Include a side salad as a starter or side dish and cook an extra portion of vegetables – fresh or frozen – to eat with dinner. Have a 'stir-fry' meal once a week.
4 Try beans, peas and pulses for a non-meat meal at least twice a week. They lend themselves to the flavours of olive oil and vegetables such as onions, garlic, tomatoes, aubergines and herbs.
5 Nuts and seeds are easily added – as a breakfast cereal 'topper', to salads, or in seed and nut snack bars – but are best limited if you are trying to lose weight!

* Note: Fresh, frozen, dried, tinned or juice all count towards the five a day.

linolenic acid (particularly walnuts). Nuts are high in fats, but mainly in the heart-healthy unsaturated fats. The one exception is coconut – this is high in saturated fat, although it is a different type from the animal-based equivalent. The jury is still out as to whether coconut oil is a suitable substitute for other saturated fats in the diet.

Legumes
Pulses such as peas, beans and lentils are excellent sources of insoluble fibre (roughage) and cholesterol-lowering soluble fibre. They are also rich in cardio-protective nutrients such as vitamin E, B vitamins, folic acid, calcium, iron and zinc. They are naturally low in fat and are a useful source of protein that can replace or extend meat or fish dishes. Dried pulses require initial soaking followed by prolonged cooking in accordance with their label so as to remove natural toxins. Tinned beans and pulses contain the same nutritional benefits.

The 'gel'-type soluble fibre found in pulses and porridge oats can bind not only dietary cholesterol, but a proportion of cholesterol-containing bile salts, preventing re-uptake for recycling by the liver, and therefore beneficially depleting the body cholesterol 'pool'. Further along the bowel, soluble fibres can act as a natural fuel source for friendly bacteria, helping to maintain a healthy bowel.

Soya beans
Soya beans deserve a special mention for their established health benefits, particularly in relation to heart disease, cancer, osteoporosis and women's health. Traditional soya foods include soya beans, miso, soya milk and oil, margarine, soy sauce, tempeh, tofu and tofu products. Soya protein concentrates, soya protein isolates and textured vegetable protein (TVP) are more modern ways of including soya in the diet.

A daily intake of 25g of soya protein can reduce LDL cholesterol by 10 per cent, sufficient to permit a UK health claim on foods that provide more than 5g of soya protein per serving. In practice, non-vegetarians often find 25g of soya protein daily difficult to achieve. For example, one soya yogurt provides 5g of soya protein, and 250ml of soya milk provides around 10g of soya protein. The benefits of soya protein appear to be dose-related – lower intakes having a lesser effect on blood cholesterol.

Not everyone appears to gain from including soya beans or soya products in their diet. Research has shown that the cholesterol-lowering benefits appear related to the level of soya protein and also the amount of soya phytochemical (called isoflavones) present in the diet. Soya isoflavones can be converted to weak oestrogens by our bowel bacteria, but only one in three of us possess the right type of bacteria to make this happen. Whether we can convert soya isoflavones or not, soya beans – like all beans – are a useful source of soluble fibre and a healthy alternative to animal protein as part of a varied diet.

Five ways to make your carbs count

Always include a 'slow' (low-GI) carb at every meal, which means:

1 Choose wholegrain cereals, porridge, or lower-sugar muesli for breakfast, or for a healthy snack.
2 Use wholemeal breads for sandwiches or toast. Try granary or high-fibre breads for variety, but use as little spread on them as possible.
3 At a main meal, fill between a quarter and a third of your plate with pasta, basmati rice or jacket potato – it's these slow-carb starchy foods that reduce hunger pangs between meals.
4 Oat-based or wholegrain bars are ideal slow-carb snacks, but can be high in sugars. Compare labels and choose those with the least amount of sugar, ideally less than 10g per serving.
5 Nuts, homemade popcorn and fresh or dried fruit are healthy between-meal snacks.

Fat calculator

Energy intake in calories	2000 kcal
Ideal goal for total fat (1/3 of total kcal)	2000 ÷ 27 = 74g fat
… of which saturated fat should not exceed…	2000 ÷ 91 = 22g saturated fat

Wholegrain cereals in the heart-healthy diet

People in Mediterranean countries tend to consume a wide variety of carbohydrate foods derived from wholegrain cereals, vegetables and legumes. Bread, pasta, rice, bulghur, couscous or potato should be included at each meal to make it filling rather than fattening.

Wholegrains such as wheat, corn, barley, oats and rye provide important cardio-protective nutrients including the B group vitamins, antioxidant vitamins, zinc and selenium. These nutrients, along with their beneficial levels of dietary fibre, confer the positive health benefits of whole grains.

Wholegrain carbohydrates provide the main dietary source of insoluble fibre (roughage), adding bulk, improving bowel function and preventing constipation. In addition, starchy foods also provide the soluble (gel-type) fibre that slows down the digestion of foods, helping to regulate appetite, improve blood glucose levels and reduce LDL cholesterol. Soluble fibre contributes to the viscosity of the food, slowing the rate of carbohydrate digestion and giving a sustained release of sugars that improve blood sugar control and increase HDL cholesterol.

The speed at which sugars are liberated from carbohydrate digestion, causing a rise in blood sugar level over a short period of time, can be gauged by the glycaemic index value of a food, also known as GI. Glycaemic load (GL) is the GI value of a food adjusted for its carbohydrate content per portion. For example, watermelon has a high GI (from fruit sugar), but each slice provides such a small amount of sugar that it has virtually no influence on blood sugar levels and so it has a very low GL rating. Low-GI/GL foods produce a modest but sustained rise in blood sugar, considered more beneficial than the rapid peak in blood sugar provided by high-GI foods. The Mediterranean diet automatically gives you a low-GI diet. 'Slow carb' – not 'low carb' – is the healthiest choice.

Oats

Oats are rich in beta-glucan, a gel-like fibre that helps to lower blood cholesterol level, to sustain blood sugar levels and to maintain bowel health. The minimum effective daily dose appears to be around 3g of beta-glucan. Oat bran provides 5.5g and rolled oats 4g of beta-glucan per 100g serving. Foods providing at least 0.75g (or a quarter) of the effective 3g dose are allowed to make a health claim on marketing literature.

Note: Beta-glucan in yeast and mushrooms is slightly different and has none of the same beneficial effects.

Fats in the Mediterranean diet

Fat is vital in our diet, providing energy, fat-soluble vitamins (vitamins A, D, E and K) and the essential fats – linoleic acid and alpha-linolenic acid – which the body cannot make. Fat is the most energy-dense nutrient in the diet, providing 9 calories per gram – that's over double the 4 kcal per gram from carbohydrates or protein. This calorie load is the same whether the fat is solid at room temperature (as in butter or lard), or liquid (as in vegetable oils). Thus the calorie load of a single wrapped butter pat is the same as that of a teaspoon of any oil – around 45 kcal. All fats should be limited if you are trying to lose weight.

Fat confers certain sensory properties, increasing the appeal of foods, affecting the taste, texture, appearance and 'mouthfeel' of a food and making it palatable. The combination of taste and energy load is probably the reason why nearly 40 per cent of the total energy in our diet comes from fat. However, too much fat, or the wrong type, increases blood cholesterol levels and background inflammation, damaging arteries and increasing the risk of heart disease.

For this reason, present guidelines recommend that around just 35 per cent of our energy should come from fat, with no more than 10 per cent of energy from saturated fat.

It's easy to calculate an ideal fat and saturated fat intake. Choose a daily calorie intake, and divide by 27 to get the grams of total fat, or by 91 for the maximum saturated fat intake each day (see table on facing page).

How are fats named?
There are three main types of fat in our food – saturated, monounsaturated and

A quick guide to fats in the diet

Type of fat	Predominant sources	Effect on blood cholesterol	Effect on inflammation
Monounsaturated	Olive oil, rapeseed (canola) oil, peanuts and peanut oil, almonds, avocado	Lowers LDL Increases HDL	Decreases inflammation
Polyunsaturated omega-3 rich	Oily fish (dark-fleshed), algae, some eggs, flaxseed (linseed), green leafy vegetables	Lowers triglycerides Lowers LDL (EPA and DHA) ALA (see page 30) – no effect	Decreases inflammation
Polyunsaturated omega-6 rich	Corn, sunflower, soya beans and soya oil, walnuts and walnut oils, safflower oils	Lowers LDL Increases HDL slightly	Increases inflammation
Saturated	Butter, lard, cheese, fatty meat, palm oil, hydrogenated fats, ice cream	Increases LDL Increases HDL	Increases inflammation
Trans fats	Hydrogenated oils found in processed foods, pastry, biscuits	Increases LDL Lowers HDL	Increases inflammation

polyunsaturated – and all dietary fats contain a mixture of the three. The names relate to their structural differences, with small variations having large health effects on cholesterol levels and inflammation. Fats are named according to the type present in the largest amount (see table above). Olive oil, for example, is classified as a monounsaturated fat even though it contains saturates and polyunsaturates, because monounsaturates make up 75 per cent of its content.

Saturated fats

Traditional diets obtained saturated fats from animal sources such as meat and dairy products, and these foods were identified by the Seven Countries Study (see page 20) as increasing cardio-vascular risk. Saturated fat increases blood cholesterol levels. The higher the saturated fat intake, the higher the blood cholesterol level. Saturated fats also increase background levels of inflam-mation, 'sensitising' the artery wall to damage.

Some foods naturally high in cholesterol (such as liver, egg yolks, prawns and shellfish) have little effect on blood cholesterol levels. This is because they contain little saturated fat, and the cholesterol they provide is offset by reduced cholesterol production by the liver.

Nowadays saturated fats are not confined to animal products. Processed foods often contain hydrogenated vegetable oils. Hydrogenation 'hardens' the oil, increasing its saturated fat content beyond that of the parent oil. In addition, the hydrogenation process can produce 'trans' fats rather than the naturally occurring 'cis' form. 'Cis' and 'trans' are terms used to describe the shape of the fat after hydrogenation. Hydrogenated cis fats can be easily used by the body, but trans fats have a different shape that the body cannot use effectively. Trans fats were not counted in the original Mediterranean diet consider-ations as the limited amount of meat and dairy foods presented very few naturally occurring trans fats. They can be found in substantial quantities in today's processed foods such as cakes, biscuits, pastries and fast foods. They are strongly related to the risk of heart disease in our modern diet, and no 'safe' level of trans fat intake has been identified.

Dairy foods

Traditionally high in fat, milk, cheese and butter were taken in small quantities in the original Mediterranean diet. However, if adding years to your life is what you are aiming for, you need healthy bones too.

How do we reconcile the need for calcium-rich foods to maintain both healthy bones and heart, with the modest dairy-food intake of the Mediterranean style of eating? The answer is to choose low-fat dairy products, widely available today, but perhaps not so fifty years ago. Low-fat versions of foods preserve their calcium whilst reducing both total and saturated fat content.

An adult requires a minimum of 700mg calcium a day, an amount that can be met in three portions of dairy food. Around 180ml of semi-skimmed or skimmed milk, or a small carton of low-fat yogurt, or a matchbox-size piece (30g) of cheese each constitutes a portion. In addition, dairy foods provide the vehicle in the UK for the addition of stanol or sterol esters, cholesterol-lowering plant extracts (see page 34). Stanol and sterol esters significantly reduce both total and LDL cholesterol levels.

Tofu, calcium-fortified soya milks and juices, the bones of tinned fish and green leafy vegetables are all good non-dairy calcium sources.

Meat and chicken

Western-style meals place a large portion of meat firmly at the centre of the meal, with vegetables and a carbohydrate as accompaniments. Meat is protein-rich but also contains saturated fat, and most of us eat more meat than is necessary to maintain health. A portion of meat, when cooked, should be approximately the same size as a deck of cards. A grilled pork chop (without fat and rind), a chicken breast, or two to three slices of roast meat are target amounts.

Remove visible fat before cooking (to avoid temptation later) and use a mono-unsaturated oil if frying. Meat and chicken lend themselves to food processing, often losing health benefits along the way. Roast chicken is much lower in calories, and total and saturated fat than chicken Kiev, and contains much less salt than processed chicken or turkey slices – so choose processed versions less often. Finally, you should try to alter the proportions of food on your plate so that the meat is the accompaniment to the vegetables, rather than the other way around.

Monounsaturated fats

Blood cholesterol levels are lowered when monounsaturated fat replaces saturated fat in the diet. Monounsaturated fats are less prone to oxidation, and this 'stable' nature extends to their role in our body – helping to prevent the destabilising of LDL cholesterol, and maintaining a neutral stance in the presence of background inflammation. For this reason they enhance the anti-inflammatory effects of omega-3 fish oils within the Mediterranean diet, in direct contrast to the omega-6-rich oils. The two main dietary sources of monounsaturated fats in the UK diet are olive oil and modified rapeseed (canola) oil, (the latter is usually sold as 'vegetable oil', but usually says on the label that it is made from rapeseed).

Cheese: percentage fat content and calorie load per serving

Type of cheese	g fat per 100g	Kcal per 30g
Cottage cheese	4	30
Ricotta cheese	11	43
Half-fat Cheddar/ hard cheese	15	82
Feta	20	75
Mozzarella	21	77
Camembert	23	87
Soya cheese	27	96
Edam	25	102
Brie	27	103
Stilton	35	123
Parmesan	30	125
Cheddar	34	125
Cream cheese	48	132

Olive oil is the main fat source in the protective Mediterranean diet. Olive oil produced in the first pressing is called 'extra virgin' olive oil, and is easily identified from its orange, yellow or green colour as derived from the native olive. The colours and flavours are important polyphenols – powerful plant antioxidants that confer additional heart-healthy benefits to this monounsaturated oil. As little as 1–2 tablespoons (15–30ml) of extra virgin olive oil daily brings significant health benefits.

Vegetable oil Rapeseed oil forms the basis of most blended vegetable oils in the UK, and is a cheap and healthy option for use in general cooking. Its neutral taste is preferred by some to the strong taste of olive oil, and its 10 per cent omega-3 fat content makes it a useful alternative.

Polyunsaturated fats

Unlike other fat types, there are two 'branches' of the polyunsaturated fatty acid family: the omega-6 and omega-3 polyunsaturated fats. The omega-6 family are found in corn, sunflower and soya bean oils and polyunsaturated spreads, and provide the essential fatty acid linoleic acid. The omega-3 fatty acids are found in some seed oils (flaxseed and rapeseed), walnuts and green, leafy vegetables; they provide the essential fatty acid alpha-linolenic acid (ALA). ALA can be converted by the body into the long-chain polyunsaturates, eicosopentanoic acid (EPA) and docosohexanoic acid (DHA), but only 10–15 per cent of ALA is usually converted. EPA and DHA are known as the 'omega-3 fish oils', and

eating oily fish gives you these fatty acids directly. Omega-6 fats and omega-3 fats both reduce cholesterol levels, although omega-3 fats, particularly EPA and DHA, provide additional benefits for blood pressure and inflammation. Our diet generally provides an abundant omega-6 intake (from oils and spreads), but is inadequate in omega-3 fats due to their being present in relatively few foods. It is important to include both fish and plant sources of omega-3 fats in the diet in order to obtain sufficient to balance the effects of omega-6 fats.

From the 1980s, sunflower and corn oils and margarines (rich in omega-6 polyunsaturates) were considered a healthy, cholesterol-free alternative to butter and lard. In more recent years, however, a high intake of omega-6 fats

has been shown to increase inflammation in the body, in contrast to the effects of the more 'neutral' monounsaturated fats. Changing margarine and oil from polyunsaturated to monounsaturated has a beneficial effect on inflammation and artery health, and enhances the benefits of omega-3 fats in the body.

Oily fish Including oily fish in the diet is now recognised as being one of the most powerful tools in terms of diet for preventing heart disease. It has long been recognised that communities such as the Inuit (groups living along the Arctic coast who eat fish regularly) have a much lower incidence of heart disease than non-fish eaters. Omega-3 fish oils, present in oily fish, seem to prevent potentially fatal disruption of heart rhythms, and reduce the risk of a blood clot (and the risk of a stroke, or heart attack), by thinning the blood and making it less sticky. They also reduce inflammation and stabilise the endothelium surface of the artery, protecting it from damage.

The amount required to gain these benefits is around 450mg of combined EPA and DHA daily, four times greater than the current average daily intake in the UK. This can be achieved by including two portions of fish per week, at least one of which should be oily (darker-fleshed fish). People who have already suffered a heart attack should aim to eat two to three portions of oily fish per week, yielding around 1000mg (1g) of EPA and DHA daily. Supplements may be required in order realistically to achieve this intake (see page 35).

Non-fish sources of omega-3 fats

There are other sources of omega-3 'fish oils', some naturally derived and some from fortified foods and drinks. Eggs from chickens fed a seed-rich diet can provide a useful amount of DHA, and their cholesterol content has a negligible effect on our blood cholesterol levels. Nuts (particularly walnuts) and seeds are rich in omega-3 fats. Smaller amounts occur naturally in green, leafy vegetables. Omega-3 fats are sometimes added to milks, margarines, orange juice, cereal bars and bread, and these can contribute towards the recommended intake of 450mg or more a day, but remember to check the amount provided by a typical portion of these foods.

Oil-rich fish omega-3 (EPA & DHA) content

	mg Omega-3 per portion
Mackerel	4500
Kipper	3700
Tuna – fresh	3000
Trout	2900
Salmon – fresh	2500
Herring (pickled)	2200
Pilchards – tinned	1800
Salmon, tinned	1400
Smoked salmon	1300
Mackerel – tinned	1300
Sardines – tinned	1200
Swordfish	1100
Crab – tinned in brine	600
Cod	300
Tuna – tinned	100

Non-fish sources of EPA & DHA

	mg Omega-3 per portion
Omega-3-enriched egg	500–750
Roast chicken, dark meat	330
Roast leg of lamb	240
Cheddar cheese	190
Whole milk	150
Roast chicken, light meat	130
Roast beef or pork	100
Omega-3-fortified margarines	75–160
Omega-3-fortified cow's milk	50–80
Omega-3-fortified fruit juices	70
Omega-3-enriched 'shot' drinks	60–80
Egg	60

Plant sources of omega-3 (alpha linolenic acid)

	mg ALA per portion
Flaxseed and flaxseed oil (also known as linseed and linseed oil)	1800
Walnuts	1500
Walnut oil	1300
Rapeseed oil	1000
Soya oil	800
Vegetable oil	700
Omega-3 fortified margarines	350
Baked beans	200
Spinach and green leafy vegetables	200
Peanuts	200
Corn oil	100
Egg	60

The plant version of omega-3, alpha-linolenic acid (ALA), can be converted in the body into EPA and then DHA. ALA is beneficial to the body whether or not it is converted. Some foods contain both plant and fish oil versions of omega-3 polyunsaturates, such as eggs and fortified margarines.

Vegetarian diets

Vegetarian diets range from the replacement of meat (and possibly fish and eggs) with pulses, nuts, seeds and dairy products, through to the avoidance of any product derived from animal sources (veganism). Research has failed to show any clear benefits from following a vegetarian or vegan diet in terms of lowering cardiovascular risk, despite the lower blood pressure, lower blood cholesterol levels and higher blood levels of antioxidant nutrients found in vegetarians compared to their meat-eating counterparts. Although total and LDL cholesterol levels are reduced with a vegetarian diet, the potential benefit is offset by a similar reduction in the cardio-protective HDL cholesterol levels.

Higher blood levels of the inflammatory protein homocysteine also commonly occur in vegetarians. Homocysteine is cleared from the body by processes requiring folic acid, vitamins B12 and B6. Vitamin B12 is found only in animal products and vegetarians have been shown to have low reserves of this nutrient, especially if they avoid milk, cheese and eggs. It may be useful for strict vegetarians to include in their diet vitamin B12-fortified foods, such as some breakfast cereals, fortified margarines and some vegetarian soya products, or yeast extract (such as Marmite/Vegemite).

Use the food labelling guide on pages 39–41 to assess the healthiness of processed vegetarian products; e.g., some ranges of vegetarian burgers provide a higher level of total and saturated fat than their equivalent meat products.

Alcohol

Alcohol is a small but significant feature of the Mediterranean diet. The alcohol content of drinks is measured in units and 1 UK unit is equal to 10ml alcohol (weighing 8g). Drinking 1–2 units of alcohol each day (as opposed to drinking none at all) appears to have some cardioprotective action, reducing mortality from coronary heart disease by 30–40 per cent.

Alcoholic drinks contain flavours and colours derived from the fruits and grains used to make it, and these also have antioxidant potential (such as resveratrol in red wine). However, it now appears to be the alcohol itself rather than its phytochemical content from colours and flavours that influences health, and so any alcoholic beverage will have a similar effect.

So a small but regular alcohol intake brings a number of important benefits – reducing blood 'stickiness', improving the action of insulin and, most important, helping to minimise the damage to the arteries that results from inflammation. Alcohol reduces LDL cholesterol and increases HDL cholesterol.

However, the benefits of alcohol are quickly lost at higher intakes, as alcohol is a toxin tolerable only in small quantities. For men over 40, drinking 1–2 units a day can reduce the risk of coronary heart disease but higher intakes are not associated with further benefits. A 'safe' upper limit of alcohol intake for a man is 3–4 units a day with at least two alcohol-free days. For women, a safe upper limit is 2–3 units of alcohol a day with similar 'rest' days, with 1–2 units daily appearing most cardioprotective. Pregnant women are advised to reduce alcohol intake to less than 1–2 units a week.

People with liver disease, 'alcohol-flushing' symptoms (where the skin turns red immediately after consuming alcohol), or with a personal or family history of alcohol abuse should abstain. Others can enjoy a daily drink as part of a healthy Mediterranean diet.

The traditional unit of alcohol bears little relation to current measures. For example, most pub measures of wine are now 175ml (one-fifth of a bottle), providing 2 units of alcohol per glass (see calculation, right). Similarly, premium lagers contain more alcohol per pint than basic lagers, and drinks poured at home are usually more generous than pub measures. Remember to factor this into any calculations for safe drinking.

Understanding alcohol units

I unit (10ml) of alcohol is:

½ pint (268ml) of beer, lager or cider
1 small glass (125ml) of wine
1 single measure (25ml, ⅙ gill) of spirits
1 small glass (50ml) of fortified wine, such as sherry

Calculating the number of units per drink (or: how many units in a large glass of wine?)

1 Identify the alcohol content by its volume (ABV), as indicated, for example, on a wine label as '11 per cent ABV'.

2 Divide this value by 100 to arrive at the alcohol content per 1ml of wine: 11 ÷ 100 = 0.11ml alcohol.

3 Multiply this value by the volume you are drinking: 0.11 x 180ml wine = 19.8ml alcohol.

4 19.8ml of alcohol is approximately 20ml of pure alcohol, which is 2 units per 180ml glass.

supplements in the heart-healthy diet

Can the Mediterranean diet be improved by taking supplements? Many people take supplements in the belief that they are nutritional talismans, and there is some evidence that a 'one-a-day' multivitamin and mineral supplement seems to be to some degree protective against cardio-vascular disease although the reason isn't fully known. It may be that a one-a-day supplement 'tops up' any minor deficiencies in the diet. It could also be the case that supplement users tend to be more health-conscious anyway and so they eat more healthily, do more exercise and smoke less, making it difficult to separate the effects of their lifestyle as a whole from those of the supplements.

Apart from any possible 'one-a-day' benefits, however, how do supplements in general measure up?

Niacin

Niacin (also known as nicotinic acid or vitamin B3) reduces VLDL and LDL levels and protects artery endothelium, but more importantly increases HDL levels. Doctors may prescribe extended release niacin, in a much larger amount than normally provided by diet alone. This level of niacin may cause 'facial flushing', but starting with a low dose of 500mg a day can help to prevent this. Niacin, at levels to benefit heart health (1000–2000mg a day), can increase anti-diabetic medication requirements.

Iron

Iron is essential to prevent anaemia, but it is also a highly reactive producer of free radicals, the cell-damaging chemicals produced as a by-product of our oxygen needs. Unless recommended by your doctor, iron supplements should be limited to 100 per cent RDA.

Antioxidant vitamins and minerals

LDL cholesterol can easily oxidise, increasing the risk of atherosclerosis. Diets such as the Mediterranean diet, rich in natural dietary antioxidants, protect the body against cardiovascular disease and stroke. However, the use of high dose dietary supplements of vitamins A, C, and E does not provide the same benefits as food and may reduce the effectiveness of 'statin' drugs prescribed to reduce blood cholesterol. A 'one-a-day' multivitamin and mineral with a broad range of micronutrients around the 100 per cent RDA level may be beneficial, but high dose supplements offer no biological or health benefit.

Garlic

Garlic is of course a major flavouring in Mediterranean cookery, and population studies confirm that garlic consumption reduces cardiovascular risk. Garlic in the diet seems to protect LDL cholesterol from becoming unstable through oxidation, may reduce the 'stickiness' of the blood and may help to moderate blood pressure. However, there is little consistent evidence to suggest that garlic supplements confer the same health benefits, and this is probably due to differences in extraction, tablet composition and the level of any active ingredient within.

Stanol and sterol esters

Sterols are natural plant substances found in grains, vegetables, nuts, seeds and pine tree extracts. When blended with fats they become sterol esters, also known as stanols, and have the ability to reduce LDL cholesterol by up to 20 per cent whilst preserving HDL levels. They work by blocking the uptake of dietary cholesterol and the re-uptake of cholesterol-rich bile salts that normally occurs in the bowel, increasing losses, and depleting the cholesterol 'reserve'. This is a dose-response effect, meaning that more ester confers more benefits, up to a plateau effect at around 2g a day – the optimal dose. Stanol and sterol esters work best when taken with other food, so take with your main meal of the day. They are ineffective if taken at breakfast. In the UK, stanol and sterol esters are added to dairy products (although they are not naturally present in these foods), and mini 'health drinks' (shot-size health drinks, available at supermarkets). In other countries they are added to fruit juices, cereals, chocolate and grain bars.

There is no need to take one of these drinks alongside fortified foods, and you don't need to use them if your cholesterol is in the normal range.

Amount of stanol or sterol ester needed for effective 2g/day load

- 1 bottle of a yogurt mini health drink each day or
- 3 portions of fortified foods: 10g buttery/ olive/light margarine spreads, 20–30g low-fat cream cheese spreads, single pot of low-fat yogurt, 200ml stanol-fortified milk

Fish oil

Fish oil supplements provide omega-3 fats, although the amount of 'active' EPA and DHA they contain varies enormously. The traditional 'teaspoon of cod liver oil' provides between 800 and 1400mg of EPA and DHA. Fish oil capsules contain much smaller amounts of EPA and DHA, as the capsule cannot hold more than 1ml (one-fifth of a teaspoon) of fish oil. Always read the label on supplements to confirm the amount of active fish oils present. Supplements providing EPA + DHA at doses of 700mg have significant benefits on plasma lipid profile.

Note: Fish liver oils should not be taken in pregnancy without medical advice, due to their high vitamin A content.

mediterranean diet: a lifestyle approach

Healthy Eating for Lower Cholesterol provides the knowledge and ideas to help you take control of your cholesterol levels and protect your arteries from damage. Together with the lifestyle approach discussed earlier (see pages 20–33), adopting the 'Mediterranean' style of eating will help you to get in shape, feel fitter and lower your risk of heart disease and stroke. This final section will consolidate the points discussed earlier in order to assist you in making healthy dietary choices whether you are eating out or at home.

The table below lists the top ten ways to 'Mediterraneanise' your diet. Each of these has an independently beneficial effect on your blood's cholesterol level and artery health, so the more points you adopt as part of your diet, the greater the protective benefits will be. Rather than attempting to take on the whole plan in one go, which may prove over-ambitious, why not try addressing one new aspect each week? After all, control of your cholesterol requires a life-long approach, and small steps, readily achieved, will form the foundation for a lifetime of good health. Within just ten weeks, your diet could be radically transformed for the better.

The top ten ways to 'Mediterraneanise' your diet

1 Change to extra-virgin olive oil or vegetable (rapeseed) oil, and margarines made from these (but use all fats and oils sparingly if you're overweight).

2 Include one to two portions of oily fish in your diet each week, or take a daily supplement providing at least 450–750mg of EPA plus DHA. Include other omega-3 rich foods each week.

3 Treat meat as a garnish, not the main component of a meal. An ideal portion is the size of a deck of cards (cooked weight). Fill the gaps on your plate with vegetables or salads.

4 Cook extra vegetables, or prepare side salads – you'll eat them. Keep frozen vegetables on standby as a quick, effortless and nutritious way towards achieving your 'five-a-day'.

5 Choose wholegrain cereals and breads more often – at least once a day.

6 Eat more pulses. Beans on toast, or butterbean or lentil soups with wholegrain bread, are great snack meal ideas. Add lentils, beans and peas to casseroles or serve as a side dish with the main course.

7 Have fruit, nuts or seeds for between-meal snacks.

8 Use more herbs and spices in your cookery, for extra antioxidant nutrients.

9 Enjoy a glass of wine or a small beer most days.

10 Use low-fat dairy foods for calcium benefit without the saturated fat.

Maintain a healthy weight for your height

Your body weight reflects the overall balance between your energy input (from food and drink) and energy output (for your body's needs, plus extra for physical activity). Being overweight reduces the impact of any healthy changes on cholesterol management. Check your waist-to-hip ratio (WHR) to see if you need to lose weight (see page 18). Following the advice in this book will help you to redress your energy balance and, in turn, to maintain a healthier weight.

Plan to eat regularly

'Plan' is the key word here. In our busy 24/7 lifestyle, what we choose to eat is often relegated to second place behind other, seemingly more important matters. We end up snacking on whatever comes to hand, be it chocolate, crisps, cakes or biscuits, none of which is conducive to cholesterol control. If you plan what you're eating, however, you will find that you can improve the nutritional value of your diet.

Breakfast
Get up ten minutes earlier in the morning to make time for breakfast – it boosts your metabolic rate and also your mental acuity. Best choices include:

✳ wholegrain cereals with skimmed or semi-skimmed milk

✳ wholemeal or granary toast with an olive-oil spread and yeast extract or reduced-sugar jam or marmalade.

✳ a breakfast kipper, mackerel, or an omega-3-enriched boiled or poached egg with wholemeal toast, if you have time!

✳ a wholegrain or oat-based cereal bar (with the main ingredient being the grain, and containing less than 10g of sugar

A lunch-break tip

Need to do your food shopping in your lunch break? Then eat first and shop afterwards. That way you will help to prevent those 'I deserve it' impulse buys of indulgent, high-fat treats.

per bar) with a drinking yogurt or ready-made low-fat yogurt smoothie if time is short.

It's also a good idea to have fresh or dried fruit, or a glass of fruit juice to make a start on your 'five-a-day'.

Lunch
Having a snack lunch? Best option is to take a sandwich from home, and use an ice pack if there is no fridge in your workplace. Use wholemeal or granary bread and rolls or the higher-fibre white bread spread with low-fat or mono-unsaturated-rich margarines. Great fillings include:
* tinned tuna (in brine or water) with low-calorie mayo and cucumber
* fresh or tinned salmon with salad
* omega-3-enriched hard-boiled egg with tomato
* cottage cheese or low-fat soft cheese (such as ricotta) with chopped spring onions and mixed herbs
* chicken or lean meat with salad.

Other good quick lunch options include:
* vegetable soup and a wholegrain roll
* baked beans or low-fat hummus with toast
* rice or pasta salad with plenty of vegetables and lean meat or oily fish.

If you need a snack to finish your meal, choose from the following list. Snacking

is a British way of life, but it can be made healthier so that you need not feel deprived when all around you are eating:
* Healthiest options: fresh fruit and raw vegetables such as crudités; rice cakes.
* Moderate-calorie snacks: a handful of nuts or seeds; lower-fat crisps; unsalted popcorn; dried-fruit 'snack packs'; baked wheat or rice-based snacks.
* Substantial (but healthy) snacks: fruit scones; wholewheat muffins; oatcakes; wholewheat pitta breads with lower-fat dips, such as reduced-fat hummus, or yogurt-based dips like tzatziki.

Main meal
Your main meal of the day is the cornerstone of healthy eating, and if you have children you can use this meal to give them a sound basis for lifelong healthy eating habits. If you're a 'heat and serve' cook, you should aim to cook a meal from basic ingredients once a week to start with, then build on this until at least half of your meals each week are cooked from scratch. Refer to the top ten Mediterranean ways (see page 37) as well as the tips that follow to ensure that your main meal is healthy.

Pots and pans Your cookware can help you to eat more healthily – if you use non-stick pans you can cook your food without added fat. Any way of cooking is better than frying. Steam, boil, poach, grill or barbecue foods instead. Griddles, grilling and grilling machines allow the fat to drain away from meat and fatty products. Cook roast meats on a trivet to allow the fat to run off. A non-stick wok can be used for healthy, stir-fried meals using a little oil, stock or wine.

Pulses For casseroles and stews, use less meat and add pulses to improve the nutritional profile of the meal. Add tinned beans and extra vegetables for healthier versions with texture, or lentils for a 'hidden' source of fibre and other plant benefits if family members don't like beans.

Dried lentils, peas and beans are a cheap and healthy way to improve your diet but need to be cooked according to the instructions on the packet to remove harmful substances, making them a slow addition to any meal. Cook large quantities of dried pulses, then freeze in smaller portions for convenience. You can then defrost in the microwave as needed or add straight to a casserole, suspending the cooking time until the frozen pulses have thawed. Alternatively, use the tinned versions that are 'ready to go'.

Salads Use any fruits and vegetables you like. Prepare whilst a microwave meal is cooking, or serve salad 'on the side' to accompany. A breakfast bowl of salad as

a starter is a proven way to help lose weight, by blunting your appetite for the main course. Instead of mayonnaise or full-fat salad dressings, use an oil 'spray' dressing with vinegar or lemon juice and herbs, or a low-calorie version of salad dressing.

Pastry Avoid pastry of any type – it's 50 per cent fat by weight. For savoury dishes, substitute potato topping, or lasagne sheets instead of a pastry base. For desserts, cut out the pastry completely. Lemon meringue tastes just as light and refreshing a dessert without the 'pie' base. If you are out and about, choose a baguette and soup rather than a hot pasty.

Salt Most of us take between 8 and 12g of salt a day, although the safe limit for adults is actually 6g a day. Having said that, most salt in the diet comes from processed foods rather than being added at mealtimes, so home-cooked meals can significantly lower salt intake. It's essential for people with high blood pressure to cut down on salt to reduce the risk of heart attack or stroke. Sea salt, organic, rock and flavoured salts are all salt (sodium chloride), so should be avoided. Avoid adding salt to foods, but use a low-salt substitute if you need to. Herbs and spices make great alternative flavours. Compare food labels to choose lower-salt alternatives.

To convert the sodium content of a food into the amount of salt present, multiply by 2.5: that is, 0.6g sodium = 0.6 x 2.5 = 1.5g salt.

A guide to assessing the 'per 100g' information on food labels

This is a lot, per 100g	This is a little, per 100g
20g fat	3g fat
3g saturated fat	1g saturated fat
10g sugar	2g sugar
0.5g sodium/ 1.25g salt	0.1g sodium/ 0.25g salt
3g fibre	0.5g fibre

Food labelling

In the real world, we often don't have the time to make every meal. Being able to 'read' food labels will help you to make great choices – in terms of comparing the nutritional benefits of different foods, and also in working out how they fit into your diet.

Manufacturers can decide how much nutritional information to list on their product. Some may just state the total fat content per 100g of food, for example, whereas others may include the saturated fat, or list monounsaturated, polyunsaturated, and trans fat content as well. Ingredients are always listed in descending order of content by weight.

Labelling in the UK is moving towards a 'traffic-light' guide for front-of-pack information, listing total and saturated

Sample food label: chilled chicken korma and rice meal for one

Indian foods are the most popular choice of a chilled ready meal, and the example used here is a typical supermarket one.

Ingredient	Per 100g	Per 500g pack
Energy	669 kJ	3347 kJ
	160 kcal	801 kcal
Protein	7.9g	39.5g
Carbohydrates:		
of which starch	10.6g	53.0g
of which sugars	1.5g	7.5g
Total fat:	9g	45g
of which saturates	4.0g	20.0g
of which monounsaturates	3.5g	17.5g
of which polyunsaturates	1.4g	7.0g
Fibre	1.6g	8.0g
Salt	0.5g	2.5g
of which sodium	0.2g	1.0g

GDA values for a chicken korma and rice meal

Amount per korma meal	GDA e.g. for women	% GDA from meal
801 kcal	2000 kcal	40%
45g fat	70g fat	64%
20g saturated fat	20g saturated fat	100%
7.5g sugar	50g sugar	15%
1.0g sodium	2.4g sodium	42%
2.5g salt	6g salt	42%

Guideline daily amounts (GDAs)

Nutrient	Men	Women
Energy (kcal)	2500	2000
Fat (g)	95	70
Saturated fat (g)	30	20
Sugar (g)	70	50
Sodium (g)	2.4	2.4
Equivalent to salt (g)	6	6

fats, sugar and salt content. Red, amber or green colour coding indicates whether levels of these nutrients are high, medium or low in processed foods. The more green lights the product has, the healthier it is. This sort of labelling is a useful benchmark for front-of-pack comparisons, but you should still check actual values for energy, total fat, and saturated fat to see how that food fits into your diet.

For foods eaten in small serving sizes (such as biscuits), or where the portion can be variable (such as breakfast cereals), compare the 'per 100g' information to select the healthiest option (see the guide on page 39). This is a quick and easy way to compare similar foods. If the value for a nutrient falls between the 'lot' and 'little' values, it is considered a moderate source of that nutrient.

For foods eaten as a complete portion such as the 500g chicken korma meal (see box opposite), use the 'amount per serving' to check nutritional values. For complete meals, however, it is often more useful to compare their nutritional content with Guideline Daily Amounts (or GDAs), nutritional values used by food manufacturers and retailers, based on the predicted needs of an average person eating a healthy diet.

The calorie, fat, saturated fat and salt content of a food can be compared to the GDAs to indicate how much that food contributes to the average daily intake of each nutrient. Many manufacturers now include GDAs on their nutrition label.

So how does the chicken korma ready meal rate nutritionally? First, the label shows nutritional values per 100g and per 500g pack, but as the pack is a meal for one you should just use the 500g weight to assess its nutritional content. Second, this label provides a lot of dietary information in a small table, but of particular interest are the calorie, fat, saturated fat and salt contents of this dish. Although using the GDA values would be more useful in terms of seeing how healthy it is, this isn't so easy to work out standing in a supermarket aisle!

So this ready meal provides 40 per cent of the GDA calorie intake – an ideal calorie load for a main meal. Yet the main source of the calories is the 45g of fat, which is equal to two-thirds of the guideline total daily fat intake and 100 per cent of the daily guideline for saturated fat. Choosing the 'reduced-fat' version of this meal would be a much healthier option, reducing both the total and the

saturated fat content of the meal. This meal also provides 2.5g (around ½ teaspoon) of salt, less than half the daily goal of 6g of salt, which is an acceptable level for a main meal.

Try to get into the habit of comparing one or two favourite foods each week with guideline values and choose the healthier options accordingly.

Eating out: healthy choices

Eating out is an enjoyment, both for the social experience and for the novelty of

trying foods that you may not have eaten before. The temptation is often to go for those foods that are too complex to attempt at home, but these tend to be the higher-fat, higher-calorie menu choices – and there's no food labelling to help you choose wisely.

If you eat out occasionally, enjoy your meal, drink a modest amount of alcohol and indulge. If, however, you eat out regularly – say, more than twice a week – you need to factor in health when making your choice so that you do not abandon an otherwise healthy diet. The 'Mediterranean' way can be factored into any style of cuisine – as Dan's recipes in this book demonstrate.

Your goal when eating out should simply be to select dishes with a high vegetable or salad content, served with a modest amount of meat or vegetarian equivalent, in a non-fatty sauce. Here are some tips:

✳ Choose a vegetable soup, fruit or salad starter – low-calorie and nutrient-packed – to help offset hunger. Have some bread (the browner, the better), but use it to mop up the soup or salad dressing and don't add butter.

✳ For the main course, consider how your plate should look: that is, loaded with vegetables, with meat on the side. Feel free to say 'yes' to more vegetables, and a side salad will improve vegetable intake further still. Ask for olive oil, lemon juice or oil-free dressing instead of full-fat mayonnaise for the salad.

✳ Choose low-fat carbohydrates as a sound meal base. Boiled or baked potatoes are better than either wedges, roast potatoes or chips. Boiled or steamed rice is better than fried or pilau rice. Boiled noodles and pasta make a sound base.

✳ As a rule of thumb, go for the dish with the least sauce or fried ingredients – a grilled fish dish, lean steak or chicken, or meat in a tomato-based sauce are good choices.

Foods from around the world

Greek Start with Greek or tomato salad (light on the dressing) or choose tzatziki (yogurt and cucumber appetiser) with bread. For the main course, try to avoid dishes like moussaka – these are rich

in oil, cream and cheese. Also limit your intake of fat-rich filo pastry – either savoury (as in spanakopita) or sweet (baklava). Select foods such as stuffed vine leaves (dolmades), roasted meats, or meat kebabs, served with couscous, boiled rice or pitta breads, or plaki (fish cooked in a tomato-based sauce). Choose fruit for your dessert.

Indian Traditional Indian (south Asian) meals are heavy on the oil – used to release the flavours from herbs and spices before other ingredients are added. Avoid the highest-fat options when eating out – coconut-flavoured curries such as korma are high in total and saturated fats. Pakoras and bhaji are usually deep-fried, as are samosas. Fried breads (like paratha and puri) and stuffed breads (keema nan) are also highly calorific and loaded with fat. Choose instead a limited number of poppadums or papads for your starter, with tandoori- or tikka-style meats, or tomato and onion-based sauces. Include some dahl – Indian cookery lends itself to using beans, lentils and chick-peas, and these are all good sources of fibre.

Choose plain, boiled rice rather than pilau and dosai or plain naan rather than filled varieties (keema and peshwari naan). Allow vegetable dishes to cool for a few minutes, then skim the oil layer from the surface and discard it, leaving the healthier vegetables below. Avoid ordering too many dishes, or share with a friend. Traditional Indian sweets are high in fat and sugar, so rather than the Indian ice-cream menu, go for the sorbet option or a fruit salad as low-fat alternatives.

If you are cooking Indian at home, try steam-frying the spices to release their aroma and flavour: use half the amount of oil that you would normally use to fry herbs and spices, and if they become too dry during cooking, add a splash or two of boiling water (hence the term 'steam-fry'). This will release the flavours without excessive fat or calorie load. You can add further water if you need to. Use tinned chick-peas, lentils or other pulses to boost the cholesterol-lowering effect of the vegetables.

If you are buying Indian to eat in, always choose the supermarket 'healthier option' to keep the total fat intake down. Skip the onion bhaji, samosa or pakora as a side dish and choose vegetables cooked with spices in a tomato-sauce base for a healthier option, or a side salad to keep to your five-a-day goal.

Chinese Avoid the fried spring rolls, and any other fried dishes. Wontons (steamed dumplings), boiled or steamed rice and noodles should form the base of the meal. Stir-fried and vegetable dishes are better choices than deep-fried dishes such as sweet-'n'-sour balls, pancake rolls and prawn crackers.

Italian Italian food is often considered to epitomise Mediterranean cookery, but you should still be cautious about some aspects of Italian cuisine! Choose soup, salad, fish or roasted vegetables for a starter, and pasta in a tomato- or clam-based sauce for the main course. If you fancy pizza, the thin-crust type is the least calorific, and toppings such as ham, chicken, vegetable, tuna or seafood tend to be the lowest in calories. Enjoy a side salad, but if you are overweight, do not mop up olive oil with the bread side dish – a sure way to add 150 kcal to your meal! Avoid 'filled' pastas such as cheese-filled cannelloni or meat lasagne, pasta with butter or cream, fried calamari and other fish, and Italian pastries. Choose a fruit-based dessert or sorbets rather than gâteaux or ice cream for dessert.

French Traditional French cooking uses high-fat sauces and cooking methods whereas nouvelle cuisine is more healthful by virtue of its small portion sizes. Choose meat or fish in a wine- or vegetable-based sauce, rather than in a hollandaise, mornay, bechamel or bearnaise sauce. Avoid 'au gratin' potato dishes for their high-saturated-fat cheese and cream content. Choose fruit-based desserts like oranges in Grand Marnier, or fruit salad, or meringue-based desserts rather than traditional tortes, tatins and crème caramel.

Mexican Mexican cuisine is perhaps one of the least compatible with controlling cholesterol. Heavily meat-based, it uses a variety of high-fat ingredients to create the complex hot-with-cool flavours and this makes it difficult to choose healthily. The best choices are chicken fajitas, chicken or beef enchiladas, and salads. Salsa is a tomato-based healthy dip, and guacamole – made from avocado – is a healthy but high-calorie option. Keep the nachos to nibble to a scant handful – it's amazing just how many can be eaten before a meal. Corn tortillas are lower in fat than flour tortillas. The high-fat foods to avoid where possible include sour cream and grated cheeses, refried beans, chorizo sausage, and flour tortillas such as quesadillas, chimichangas and burritos.

Fast food Avoid chips – but if you really can't resist, limit your intake. Choose the smallest burger or chicken grill, and don't go for added cheese or relishes. Choose tea, coffee, water, fruit juice, diet drinks or milk instead of high-sugar drinks and high-fat milkshakes. Do not eat the batter on fried fish and add some vegetables, such as mushy peas, baked beans or pickled onions.

Or take inspiration from Dan's recipes – and eat in instead!

from the chef

I specialise in healthy eating and always want to make it fresh, easy and interesting. I have been very lucky to work in many countries across Asia and Europe. The Mediterranean is a huge inspiration and, wonderfully, this style of cooking is recognised as being one of the most healthy too. I have included lots of simple and delicious fish recipes, which I hope will inspire those who are unused to cooking with fish. I like to use ingredients that are easy to find, as well as experimenting with new ideas, but I do not try to 're-invent the wheel' as there are so many dishes out there that are classic and do not need change. Presentation is important and I enjoy creating dishes that appeal to the eye as well as the tastebuds.

It is vital to keep cholesterol under control, and happily a balanced diet can make a real difference. In this book I hope you will see foods you love, want to make the dishes and not feel that you are compromising on flavour by not eating foods high in saturated fats. After losing weight myself I never use butter or cream in my recipes, but I never feel deprived. Think not only of olive oil but also of other interesting oils that are low in saturated fat, like sesame oil and walnut oil. Fresh herbs and spices are also a great way to liven up the simplest of dishes, from basil and mint to ginger, chilli and lemongrass; you will see how you can get food to explode with flavour and then you will never miss the fat.

Always try to fuel your body with the right things and you will instantly feel the benefit. If it can be done in a tasty, easy way I think you will be halfway there!

1

breakfasts and brunches

more than muesli

This recipe is for homemade muesli but you could substitute ready-made muesli and add the maple syrup, milk and yogurt. Perfect for a Sunday brunch, served in large wine glasses.

200g jumbo porridge oats
25g flaked bran or wheat germ
75g barley or rye flakes
50g hazelnuts, lightly crushed
50g flaked almonds
50g raisins
50g dried apricots, chopped
4–6 tablespoons maple syrup
50–75ml semi-skimmed milk
4 tablespoons low-fat Greek yogurt

Serves 4–6

Mix all the ingredients together well in a large mixing bowl. Refrigerate overnight. (You may need to add more milk to keep the right consistency as the muesli absorbs most of the liquid.) Those with a sweet tooth may want to top with more maple syrup!

PER SERVING:
547 KCALS, 20.4G FAT, 2.5G SATURATED FAT, 0.04G SODIUM

energiser smoothie

A great breakfast for people on the go. Make it the night before and take it with you to work; it will fill you up and give you a steady supply of energy throughout the morning.

2 bananas
300ml skimmed milk
150ml fresh orange juice
250g low-fat yogurt
200g fresh strawberries
1 tablespoon honey
1 teaspoon ground cinnamon
4 passion fruit

Serves 4

Well, not too much to this one – just put all the ingredients except the passion fruit in a blender and whizz until smooth.

When ready to serve just spoon some passion fruit seeds over the top.

This can be kept in the fridge for at least a day, so make the night before to have on hand the next morning. Another tip is to use fruit that is about to 'turn' – it works well and is a great way to avoid wasting expensive fruit.

PER SERVING:
154 KCALS, 1.1G FAT, 0.6G SATURATED FAT, 0.09G SODIUM

buckwheat pancakes

These are American-style pancakes but made with buckwheat flour, which has a delicious flavour. Try adding fresh fruit to the batter for extra sweetness.

165g buckwheat flour
2 teaspoons brown sugar
1 teaspoon baking powder
4 eggs
500ml skimmed milk
2 tablespoons vegetable (rapeseed) oil
Fresh fruit and maple syrup, to serve

Serves 4–6

Mix together in a large bowl the flour, sugar and baking powder.

Now crack in the eggs and add the milk. Whisk with a hand whisk until smooth.

Heat some of the oil in a frying pan over a medium heat. Drop a generous tablespoon of the batter into the pan and cook until bubbles appear (around 2 minutes), then flip over and cook for a further 30 seconds. Repeat with the remaining oil and batter.

Serve the pancakes with fresh fruit and maple syrup.

PER SERVING:
326 KCALS, 12G FAT, 2.1G SATURATED FAT, 0.27G SODIUM

breakfast bars

These make a great start to the day, especially if you need breakfast on the go. Bake ahead of time and take with you to work. You can use any combination of dried fruit, nuts and seeds.

90g dried figs
90g dried apricots
90g dried pears
50g sunflower seeds
50g cashew nuts
60g porridge oats
60g wholemeal flour
60ml fresh orange juice
3 tablespoons runny honey

Makes 22–24

Preheat the oven to 190°C/375°F/gas mark 5. Grease a 20cm square shallow baking tray.

Place the fruit in a blender and blend until roughly chopped. Add the sunflower seeds, cashew nuts, oats and flour and mix in well but do not blend.

Now add the juice and honey and blend roughly. Transfer the mix into the baking tray and bake in the oven for 20–25 minutes or until golden brown.

Take out of the oven and allow to cool before slicing into bars.

PER BAR:
79 KCALS, 2.8G FAT, 0.4G SATURATED FAT, 0.01G SODIUM

banana porridge

Porridge is good with any fruit, but if you put bananas at the bottom of the bowl the porridge warms them – lovely on a cold winter morning! You can use any toasted seeds for the topping.

2 bananas, sliced
110g porridge oats
275ml semi-skimmed milk
2–3 tablespoons maple syrup or runny honey
2 tablespoons sunflower seeds, toasted in a dry frying pan

Serves 4

Divide the banana slices between 4 small bowls.

Place the oats and milk in a pan, mix well and bring to the boil. Stir as the porridge thickens. After about 5 minutes, when the porridge has thickened, pour into serving bowls.

Drizzle with maple syrup or honey and serve sprinkled with the sunflower seeds.

PER SERVING:
238 KCALS, 6.2G FAT, 1.4G SATURATED FAT, 0.03G SODIUM

scrambled eggs and smoked salmon

There is nothing quite like wild salmon from Scottish or Atlantic waters, and the fact it is good for you makes it better still!

6 eggs plus 2 egg whites
Drizzle of vegetable
(rapeseed) oil
450g Scottish smoked salmon
Bunch of fresh chives, chopped

Serves 4

In a large bowl whisk together the eggs and the egg whites.

Heat a drizzle of oil in a large non-stick pan. Add the eggs and cook on a medium-low heat, gently and continuously pulling them into the centre of the pan. This allows the eggs to cook without burning.

Remove from the heat when the eggs are still a little runny as they will continue to cook with the heat of the pan and you do not want to overcook them.

Serve with smoked salmon and chopped chives.

PER SERVING:
291 KCALS, 14.7G FAT, 3.7G SATURATED FAT, 2.25G SODIUM

sweetcorn cakes with dipping sauce

Perfect for a Sunday brunch. Serve with Thai dipping sauce for an Eastern twist, or alternatively with salsa to give a Mexican flavour.

500g tinned sweetcorn, drained
1 small onion
1 egg plus 1 egg white
Handful of fresh coriander, plus extra to garnish
125g plain flour
1 teaspoon baking powder
Freshly ground black pepper
2 tablespoons vegetable (rapeseed) oil
Thai dipping sauce or salsa (see page 135), to serve

Serves 4–6

Put all the ingredients (except for 100g of the sweetcorn and the oil) in a blender and blend until smooth.

Mix the remaining corn in by hand.

Heat the oil in a frying pan.

Form large spoonfuls of the mix into patties and fry, 4 at a time, cooking for 2 minutes on each side.

Transfer to a serving plate, garnish with coriander and serve the Thai dipping sauce or salsa on the side.

PER SERVING (WITHOUT DIPPING SAUCE):
311 KCALS, 8.6G FAT, 1G SATURATED FAT, 0.46G SODIUM

mexican breakfast burrito

Here is a Mexican recipe fit for any weekend brunch; it's always a winner when you need something filling and satisfying. It's easy to prepare ahead of time and can be served at room temperature.

400g tin refried beans
4 large flour tortillas
150g reduced-fat Cheddar cheese, grated
100g low-fat fromage frais
2 tablespoons semi-skimmed milk
1 small red chilli, finely chopped
Freshly ground black pepper
1 tablespoon vegetable (rapeseed) oil

Serves 4

Preheat the oven to 200°C/400°F/gas mark 6.

Drain the beans and mash them.

Put each tortilla on a large sheet of foil, spread with the mashed beans and add the cheese. Fold the foil over the top and seal, keeping it flat, then put in the oven and cook for 8–10 minutes. Remove from the oven and set aside.

Mix the fromage frais, milk and chilli in a bowl and season with black pepper.

Open the foil parcels and spoon the fromage frais mixture on top of the burritos, dividing it equally between them.

This can also be served with salsa or tofu guacamole (see page 135).

PER SERVING:
381 KCALS, 19.1G FAT, 8.7G SATURATED FAT, 0.93G SODIUM

congee

This dish is eaten all over Asia. It's perfect to start the day with (especially when the weather is cold) as the rice releases energy slowly through the morning. Steamed chicken may be added for a more filling dish.

2.5 litres vegetable stock, homemade (see page 138)
  or made with low-salt stock cubes
300g white rice (short-grain is perfect)
250ml water
2 hard-boiled eggs, quartered
6 spring onions, very finely chopped
2 tablespoons reduced-salt soy sauce

Serves 4–6

Put the stock in a pan and bring to the boil.

Rinse the rice in a sieve to wash away any starch, then add to the stock, lowering the heat to a gentle simmer. Cook for 1 hour, adding the water about 20 minutes into the cooking time. Stir a few times throughout the cooking time, adding more water if needed.

Spoon into soup bowls and add a couple of egg quarters, chopped spring onions and a drizzle of soy sauce to each one.

PER SERVING:
403 KCALS, 4.6G FAT, 0.8G SATURATED FAT, 0.65G SODIUM

dried fruit muffins

Any dried fruits will work, from raisins to apricots. You could also try adding a mixture of nuts to the batter. Serve with freshly squeezed orange juice and enjoy!

1 teaspoon vegetable (rapeseed) oil
8 tablepoons caster sugar
200g mixed dried fruit
4 tablespoons wholemeal flour
2 eggs
150ml semi-skimmed milk

Serves 4 (makes about 12 muffins)

Preheat the oven to 190°C/375°F/gas mark 5. Grease 12 muffin moulds with vegetable oil.

Heat 6 tablespoons of caster sugar in a heavy-based pan until it dissolves. Add the dried fruit, stir in and set aside.

Place the flour and remaining sugar into a bowl. Whisk in the eggs and then add the milk, whisking to form a thick batter.

Pour the batter into the pan with the dried fruit and sugar mix, then divide among the muffin moulds. Bake in the oven for 10–15 minutes.

Allow to cool and serve.

PER MUFFIN:
121 KCALS, 1.6G FAT, 0.4G SATURATED FAT, 0.03G SODIUM

spanish omelette

This is an easy dish to make. If you have any left over, keep in the fridge and save for later – it is good cold as well as hot. Add a variety of whatever vegetables are in season, to suit your own taste.

2 tablespoons olive oil or vegetable (rapeseed) oil,
  plus extra for greasing
3 large potatoes, very thinly sliced
1 large onion, thinly sliced
6 eggs
½ teaspoon paprika
Freshly ground black pepper
Dash of Tabasco sauce

Serves 6

Preheat the oven to 150°C/300°F/gas mark 2. Use the oil to grease a 22 x 30cm baking tray.

Heat the oil in a large frying pan and cook the potatoes until nearly soft, then add the onion and cook until it is transparent. Turn into a large bowl and set aside to cool.

Lightly beat the eggs and pour over the potatoes and onion. Add the paprika, pepper and Tabasco sauce and mix well.

Tip the mixture into the baking tray and cook in the oven for about 35 minutes until the centre is cooked (it should wobble when shaken). Alternatively, if your frying pan has an oven-proof handle, pour the mixture back into the frying pan, cook for a few minutes over a low heat, then place in the oven for 30 minutes.

Cut into pizza-style wedges and serve.

PER SERVING: 2
02 KCALS, 10.1G FAT, 2.1G SATURATED FAT, 0.08G SODIUM

steamed dim sum

Dim sum is a traditional Sunday breakfast all across China. It's actually very easy to make, so why not give it a go? For a vegetarian version, use cabbage, mushrooms and water chestnuts instead of meat.

450g lean minced chicken
450g lean minced pork
1 egg white
1 tablespoon reduced-salt soy sauce, plus extra for dipping
2 garlic cloves
2.5cm cube fresh ginger
1 tablespoon sesame oil
5 spring onions, finely chopped
1–2 packs won ton wrappers

Serves 8–10

Put all the ingredients apart from the spring onions and won ton wrappers in a food processor. Blend to a rough paste. Add the chopped spring onions.

Now take a won ton sheet and place a tablespoon of the mixture on to the centre. Moisten the edges with water and crimp them all the way round, making an open parcel. Repeat with the rest of the wrappers and mixture. (You could also try crimping the edges to make closed parcels.)

Put the parcels in a single or double steamer (or a bamboo steamer) and steam for 8–10 minutes.

Serve with soy sauce.

PER SERVING:
222 KCALS, 5.8G FAT, 1.7G SATURATED FAT, 0.36G SODIUM

fresh salmon kedgeree

A traditional breakfast simplified and with much of the fat removed. Salmon adds a milder flavour to this dish than traditional kippers, but still provides the healthy omega-3 fats.

1 tablespoon vegetable (rapeseed) oil
1 large onion, finely chopped
2 garlic cloves, crushed
1kg cooked white rice (any rice will work with this)
Water and vinegar, for cooking the eggs
4 eggs
500g fresh salmon fillet
Dash of paprika
Freshly ground black pepper
Handful of fresh parsley, chopped

Serves 4

In a large pan or wok, heat the oil and add the onion. Cook on a medium heat for 5 minutes, trying not to let the onion brown. Add the garlic, then the rice and toss well. Remove from the heat.

Meanwhile, in a pan, heat two thirds water to one third vinegar (white wine or rice vinegar is best). When it is boiling hard add 2 of the eggs and poach for 2 minutes. Remove from the pan and add to a bowl of cold water to stop the cooking process. Repeat with the remaining 2 eggs.

Heat a non-stick pan and add the salmon. You don't need oil when cooking salmon in a non-stick pan as it releases its own oils. Cook over a medium heat for 3–4 minutes on each side. Return the rice pan to the heat and add the salmon to it, flaking it as you mix it in well with the rice mixture. Add paprika and freshly ground pepper to taste. Remove from the heat after a minute or so and mix in the parsley.

Divide the mixture between 4 bowls, placing a poached egg on each, and serve.

PER SERVING:
654 KCALS, 23.1G FAT, 4.5G SATURATED FAT, 0.13G SODIUM

2

soups and salads

butternut squash soup

The butternut has such a rich flavour that you end up with a filling soup and a silky texture even without the oil, butter or cream that is so often used in soups.

1 medium butternut squash
1 tablespoon olive oil
1 onion, diced
1 small potato, quartered
2 garlic cloves
Salt and freshly ground black pepper
850ml vegetable stock, homemade (see page 138)
  or made with low-salt
stock cubes
Handful of chives, chopped

Serves 4–6

Peel the butternut squash, scoop out the seeds and cut the flesh into thick wedges.

Heat the oil in a large pan, then add the onion and cook on a low heat for 1–2 minutes.

Add the butternut and potato and coat in the oil. Cook for 2 minutes on a medium heat. Add the garlic and season. Now add the stock and simmer for 25 minutes.

Using a hand blender or food-processor, blend thoroughly. To serve, sprinkle with some chopped chives.

PER SERVING:
168 KCALS, 3.3G FAT, 0.4G SATURATED FAT, 0.27G SODIUM

chilled avocado soup

Avocados are rich in healthier monounsaturated fat. This yummy soup can also be made into a dipping sauce for asparagus or artichokes (use 3 tablespoons of stock per each half avocado).

4 rashers bacon
2 ripe avocados
1.5 litres vegetable or chicken stock, homemade (see pages 138 and 139) or made with low-salt stock cubes
2 tablespoons plain low-fat yogurt
Juice of ½ lemon
Freshly ground black pepper

Serves 4

Remove all the fat from the bacon rashers – I do this with scissors – and cut the bacon into thin strips. Fry in a pan on a medium heat until brown.

Meanwhile, in a blender, whizz the avocados, stock, yogurt and lemon juice until smooth and season with black pepper.

Serve chilled, or at room temperature, garnished with the strips of bacon.

PER SERVING:
220 KCALS, 14.1G FAT, 2G SATURATED FAT, 0.56G SODIUM

sweetcorn and lemongrass soup

Lemongrass is widely used in Thai cuisine and has a lemony aroma. This soup is easy to make and can be kept for up to a week in the fridge.

10–12 lemongrass stalks
8–10 corn cobs
2 tablespoons vegetable (rapeseed) oil
1 large onion, finely chopped
1 garlic clove, crushed
2.4 litres vegetable stock, homemade (see page 138) or made with low-salt stock cubes
Handful of fresh chives, chopped

Serves 8

Peel the lemongrass stalks until you get to the tender white parts that are easy to cut without fraying. Now finely chop them and set aside.

Using a knife, slice the corn kernels off the cobs and put in a bowl, reserving 3 tablespoons of kernels for garnishing.

Heat the oil in a large stock pot and add the onion, cooking for 2–3 minutes. Add the prepared lemongrass, crushed garlic and bowl of corn kernels. Stir for a minute and add the stock. Simmer for 20–25 minutes on a low heat.

Meanwhile, heat a frying pan with a drizzle of olive oil and fry the reserved corn kernels for a few minutes until crispy and golden brown.

When the soup is ready, put in a blender and whizz until smooth.

Serve topped with a few fried corn kernels and a sprinkling of chopped chives.

PER SERVING:
187 KCALS, 4.9G FAT, 0.2G SATURATED FAT, 0.15G SODIUM

gazpacho

A Spanish classic that you do not always see on a menu these days, which is a shame. It gets better over time, so keep in the fridge for a few days. Delicious on a spring or summer day.

Handful each of:
   fresh chives
   fresh tarragon
   fresh parsley
   fresh basil
   fresh marjoram
2 garlic cloves, crushed
1 red pepper, diced
4 large tomatoes, peeled, deseeded and diced
Juice of 1 lemon
425ml vegetable stock, made with a low-salt stock cube, cooled
150ml tomato juice
1 onion, finely chopped
1 small red chilli
½ cucumber, finely chopped
Freshly ground black pepper

Serves 4–6

Chop the herbs and mix with the crushed garlic.

Add the red pepper and tomatoes to the herbs and also the lemon juice. Add the cold stock and the tomato juice.

Add the onion, red chilli and cucumber to the soup. Season with black pepper and chill for at least 4 hours before serving.

PER SERVING:
67 KCALS, 0.9G FAT, 0.1G SATURATED FAT, 0.12G SODIUM

hearty fish soup

Try this with any fish and add seafood if you wish. There really are no boundaries as every kind of fish and seafood will work. Very warming on a winter's day.

1–2 tablespoons olive oil
1 garlic clove, crushed
850ml fish stock, homemade (see page 139), or made with low-salt stock cubes
225g halibut, roughly chopped
225g cod, roughly chopped
225g swordfish, roughly chopped
8 small scallops
6 medium tomatoes, quartered
1 tablespoon tomato paste
Handful of fresh chives, chopped
4 spring onions, sliced

Serves 6–8

Heat the oil in a large pan on a medium heat, throw in the garlic and turn for 30 seconds.

Add the stock, followed by all the fish, the tomatoes and tomato paste and boil for 5–8 minutes. It's that simple!

Serve garnished with chopped chives and sliced spring onions.

PER SERVING:
193 KCALS, 5.2G FAT, 0.8G SATURATED FAT, 0.24G SODIUM

spicy thai soup

The traditional tom yum soup uses the herbs and spices whole; I like to chop them finely so that you can eat all the soup. It really is the chicken soup of the East. So easy to make and the aroma is wonderful.

1 garlic clove, crushed
2 tablespoons Thai fish sauce
3 small red chillies, including seeds for spice
2–3 lemongrass stalks, finely chopped
2.5cm cube fresh ginger
1½ teaspoons Thai chilli paste
180ml vegetable stock, homemade (see page 138) or made with low-salt stock cubes
6 lime leaves (kaffir, dried or fresh)
900g boneless chicken, skinned and cut into strips
225g mixed mushrooms
Handful of fresh coriander, chopped

Serves 4–6

Put the garlic, fish sauce, chillies, lemongrass, ginger and chilli paste in a blender and whizz to a smooth paste.

Put the stock in a pan and bring to the boil, then add the ingredients from the blender, together with the lime leaves, and simmer for 10 minutes.

Add the chicken and mushrooms and cook for another 20 minutes on a low heat.

Serve garnished with chopped coriander.

PER SERVING:
278 KCALS, 5.3G FAT, 1.6G SATURATED FAT, 0.81G SODIUM

chicken soup

This dish is made all over the world. The Chinese make it for maintaining good strength and it has been known as 'the Jewish penicillin' for centuries. It is very satisfying.

1 tablespoon olive oil or vegetable (rapeseed) oil
2 onions, diced
2 sticks celery, finely chopped
2 carrots, finely diced
55g plain flour
1.2 litres chicken stock, homemade (see page 139)
    or made with low-salt stock cubes
Freshly ground black pepper
450g boneless cooked chicken, skinned and shredded
1 tablespoon chopped parsley

Serves 6

Heat the oil in a large saucepan. Add the onions, celery and carrots and cook for 3–4 minutes on a low heat.

Stir in the flour and cook for 1 minute, then add the chicken stock and bring to the boil. Season with black pepper and simmer for 10 minutes.

Add the cooked chicken and heat through for 5 minutes, then serve, garnished with parsley.

PER SERVING:
244 KCALS, 8G FAT, 2.2G SATURATED FAT, 0.17G SODIUM

mixed herb salad

This salad is full of flavour, so you will not need much dressing to make it tasty. The best way to dress a salad is to put all of the salad ingredients in a large bowl, then add the dressing and toss well.

1 Cos lettuce
1 iceberg lettuce
12 cherry tomatoes, halved
½ cucumber, diced
Handful each of:
    fresh basil
    fresh coriander
    fresh tarragon
    fresh parsley

For the dressing
6 tablespoons extra virgin olive oil
1 tablespoon Dijon mustard
Juice and grated zest of 1 lemon
½ garlic clove, crushed

Serves 4

Cut up the lettuces and put in a bowl. Add the tomatoes and cucumber.

Now chop the herbs roughly and set aside.

In a different bowl, whisk together the olive oil, mustard, lemon juice and zest and the garlic. Add the herbs, then use to dress the salad. Serve immediately.

PER SERVING:
196 KCALS, 17.9G FAT, 2.4G SATURATED FAT, 0.12G SODIUM

chickpea and bean salad

This has a wonderful Mediterranean feel to it and works equally well as a side dish or a lunch-time salad. It also makes a great partner to fish dishes.

150g tin chickpeas
150g tin red kidney beans
150g tin butter beans
Juice and grated zest of 1 lemon
1 garlic clove, crushed
2 tablespoons extra virgin olive oil
Handful of fresh basil leaves
Freshly ground black pepper

Serves 4

Drain the chickpeas and beans and mix well in a large bowl. Add the lemon juice and the garlic.

Add the olive oil and mix well.

Now shred the basil leaves and add to the bowl, together with the zest of the lemon. Season with black pepper and give another mix.

Refrigerate overnight for all the flavours to strengthen before you serve the salad.

PER SERVING:
119 KCALS, 6.4G FAT, 0.8G SATURATED FAT, 0.22G SODIUM

four-mushroom salad with truffle oil

White truffle oil is an infused oil normally made with olive oil. The smell is fabulous and the oil is low in saturated fat.

700g mushrooms (4 varieties –
   I like shiitake, portobello, oyster and wild)
6 tablespoons extra virgin olive oil
1 garlic clove, crushed
Freshly ground black pepper
225g rocket leaves
Juice of 1 lemon
4 tablespoons white truffle oil
Fresh basil leaves to serve

Serves 4

Cut the mushrooms into large wedges and cook in a large pan with 3 tablespoons of the olive oil.

Add the garlic and cook on a medium heat for around 5 minutes.

Season with black pepper, then remove from the heat and set aside to cool.

In a mixing bowl, mix the rocket leaves, lemon juice and remaining olive oil. Season with black pepper and mix well. Add the mushrooms to the bowl and mix well again.

Divide between 4 serving plates, drizzle a tablespoon of white truffle oil over each one, garnish with fresh basil leaves and serve.

PER SERVING:
295 KCALS, 28.3G FAT, 3.2G SATURATED FAT, 0.06G SODIUM

rocket and tuna salad

Rocket has such a rich flavour and it is also very good for you in all the same ways as spinach. Serve with some fresh bread to mop up the delicious juices.

4 fresh medium tuna steaks, around 3cm thick
6 tablespoons extra virgin olive oil
1 teaspoon English mustard
1 tablespoon white wine vinegar
150g rocket leaves
8 sun-dried tomatoes, roughly chopped
Freshly ground black pepper

Serves 4

In a hot pan, heat 1 tablespoon of the olive oil. Now sear 2 of the tuna steaks for 1 minute on each side. Cook the remaining 2 steaks in the same way and set them all aside. They will be rare, but this is the best way to eat fresh tuna.

In a bowl, whisk the remaining oil with the mustard and vinegar.

Put the rocket leaves and sun-dried tomatoes in a large mixing bowl, then add the dressing. Season with black pepper and mix again.

Divide the salad between 4 plates and top each with a tuna steak, cut in half at an angle and pointing upwards on the salad.

PER SERVING:
376 KCALS, 23.9G FAT, 3.9G SATURATED FAT, 0.16G SODIUM

classic french salad

The French are so adventurous with their salads, using a huge variety of ingredients to make every bite different. Here is a classic French salad.

A little olive oil
6 bacon rashers
1 egg
4 slices thick white bread, cut into 5mm cubes
4 Romaine lettuce heads
75g fresh spinach
Freshly ground black pepper

For the dressing
Juice of ½ lemon
1 teaspoon Dijon mustard
A few fresh basil leaves, shredded
3 tablespoons extra virgin olive oil

Serves 4

Make the dressing by mixing the lemon juice, mustard, basil and olive oil together well.

Now remove the fat from the bacon and cut the strips into 1cm cubes.

In a hot pan, heat a drizzle of oil and add the bacon. Cook on a medium heat until brown, then remove from the pan and set aside.

Poach the egg and set aside.

Add the cubed bread to the pan you used to cook the bacon and fry for a few minutes with a little more oil until crispy.

Cut up the lettuce heads and place in a large mixing bowl with the spinach. Pour on the dressing and mix very well with your hands. Add the croûtons, bacon, poached egg and black pepper and serve.

PER SERVING:
291 KCALS, 17.2G FAT, 2.9G SATURATED FAT, 0.72G SODIUM

fresh tuna niçoise

Using fresh tuna in this dish really makes a difference, although tinned may be used as a substitute. This is a modern twist on the French classic and is a meal in itself.

12 new potatoes
4 tablespoons olive oil
Freshly ground black pepper
2 garlic cloves, crushed, plus 1 small whole garlic clove
30 French beans
8 quails' eggs

1 tin pitted black olives (225g, drained)
3 tablespoons lemon juice
2 teaspoons Dijon mustard
1 tail end of fresh tuna (enough to be cut into 3 x 5cm slices per person)

Serves 4

Preheat the oven to 190°C/375°F/gas mark 5. Put the new potatoes in an ovenproof dish and add a little of the olive oil, plenty of black pepper and the crushed garlic. Mix well, then put in the oven and cook for 20–30 minutes, stirring occasionally.

Put the French beans in a pan of boiling water and boil for 15 minutes. Drain, then run them immediately under cold water to keep their colour. Set aside. Put the quails' eggs in a pan of boiling water and boil for a few minutes. Drain, peel, set aside.

Put the olives, half of the lemon juice and the small garlic clove in a blender and whizz to a lumpy paste. (May be done with a hand-held blender.) Mix the remaining olive oil, the Dijon mustard and the remaining lemon juice in a dish to make a dressing. Set aside.

Heat a tiny amount of olive oil in a pan (just enough to prevent sticking) and, when it is hot, add the tuna end in one piece. Fry on a high heat for about 15 seconds on each side and remove from the pan.

Slice the tuna into 5cm wheels, putting 3 on each plate. Add the potatoes, followed by the beans. Using spoons, make a quenelle of (what is now) the olive tapenade and add to the plates. Drizzle the dressing over the beans. Halve the quails' eggs, add to each salad and serve.

PER SERVING:
456 KCALS, 28.5G FAT, 3.7G SATURATED FAT, 0.47G SODIUM

thai chicken salad

A very simple way to recreate all the flavours of Thailand without deep-frying the chicken. This dressing can be used for other salads too: it instantly adds zing!

4 chicken breasts, skinless
1 tablespoon vegetable (rapeseed) oil
1 small bird's eye chilli, finely chopped, not deseeded
2.5cm cube fresh ginger, grated
2 lemongrass stalks, peeled and finely chopped
1 tablespoon chopped fresh mint
1 tablespoon brown sugar
1 garlic clove, crushed
Juice of 1 lemon
1 tablespoon reduced-salt soy sauce
1 tablespoon Thai fish sauce
150g fresh spinach
Lime wedges, to serve

Serves 4

Slice the chicken breasts into 2.5cm pieces.

Heat the oil in a pan and fry the chicken on a medium–high heat until it is cooked through. Try not to keep turning the chicken in the pan so that it gets a nice, caramelised glaze.

Meanwhile, put the chilli, ginger, lemongrass, mint, sugar, lemon juice, garlic, soy sauce and fish sauce in a bowl and mix together very well.

Add the cooked chicken to the bowl and mix again.

Now add the spinach (uncooked), mix well and serve as a salad at once, with lime wedges on the side.

PER SERVING:
206 KCALS, 4.6G FAT, 0.7G SATURATED FAT, 0.7G SODIUM

chicken liver salad

Liver is rich in iron and chicken livers contain little fat. Do note, however, that women considering pregnancy or in the early stages of pregnancy should avoid liver.

Salad leaves of your choice
150g spinach
1 tablespoon vegetable (rapeseed) oil
1 small onion, finely chopped
450g chicken livers
1 teaspoon wholegrain mustard
2 tablespoons balsamic vinegar
Salt and freshly ground black pepper

Serves 4

Slice the salad leaves and put in a bowl with the spinach.

Heat the oil in a large pan, add the onion and cook on a medium heat for 2 minutes.

Now sear the chicken livers in the same pan on a high heat, then reduce the heat and cook through: this should take 3–4 minutes. Add the mustard and the balsamic vinegar, remove from the heat and mix well.

Season and pour over the salad and serve on individual serving plates.

PER SERVING:
153 KCALS, 6G FAT, 1.1G SATURATED FAT, 0.26G SODIUM

3

sides, snacks and starters

baked garlic

Don't be wary of the garlic, as when you cook it most of the pungency disappears. I love this on toasted ciabatta or other fresh, warm bread.

1 garlic bulb
Extra virgin olive oil
Few sprigs of fresh rosemary

Serves 6

Preheat the oven to 160°C/325°F/gas mark 3. Cut through the middle of the garlic bulb and drizzle with oil. Stuff with the rosemary sprigs, push the two halves back together and wrap in foil. Put in the oven and cook for 35 minutes.

PER SERVING:
16 KCALS, 0.9G FAT, 0.1G SATURATED FAT, 0G SODIUM

roasted butternut squash and garlic

This is great served with roast chicken.

4 medium butternut squash
4–6 tablespoons extra virgin olive oil
Freshly ground black pepper
Pinch of cayenne pepper
1 garlic bulb

Serves 4–6

Preheat the oven to 220°C/425°F/gas mark 7. Peel the butternut squash using a potato peeler. Scoop out the seeds with a spoon and discard, then cut the flesh into 5cm wedges. Put in a mixing bowl with 3 tablespoons of the olive oil and mix well. Season with black pepper and cayenne pepper and mix again, then transfer into an ovenproof dish. Now break up the garlic bulb into single cloves. Do not peel. Add the cloves to the butternut and roast in the oven for 45 minutes. Add more oil if needed.

PER SERVING:
222 KCALS, 11.4G FAT, 1.5G SATURATED FAT, 0.01G SODIUM

roast potatoes with sage

These potatoes can be eaten as a snack or with a Sunday roast such as Italian-style Roast Chicken (see page 113) or Saffron Chicken (see page 114).

6 baking potatoes
4 tablespoons extra virgin olive oil or vegetable (rapeseed) oil
Handful of fresh sage leaves, roughly chopped
Freshly ground black pepper

Serves 4

Preheat the oven to 220°C/425°F/gas mark 7. Peel and quarter the potatoes. Place in a pan of boiling water for 5 minutes, drain and place on a baking tray. Add the oil and the sage leaves to the tray. Mix all the ingredients together and season well with black pepper. Place in the oven and cook for 50 minutes, turning them every 15 minutes to ensure even cooking.

PER SERVING:
327 KCALS, 11.7G FAT, 1.6G SATURATED FAT, 0.02G SODIUM

low-fat chunky chips

Very simple to make and so delicious you will forget that they are not deep-fried. Serve with any of the salad recipes or main dishes in this book.

5 large baking potatoes
4 tablespoons extra virgin olive oil or vegetable (rapeseed) oil
Rock salt

Serves 4

Preheat the oven to 180°C/350°F/gas mark 4. Peel the potatoes and cut into large chips around 2.5cm thick.
Put the chips in a large bowl and add the oil. Give them a good mix (using your hands works best). Line a baking tray with foil and lay the chips on it. Sprinkle with rock salt and cook in the oven for 30 minutes, giving them a good turn halfway through the cooking time so that they brown on all sides.

PER SERVING:
286 KCALS, 11.5G FAT, 1.6G SATURATED FAT, 0.21G SODIUM

japanese-style beans

What a wonderful way to jazz up green beans! Make sure that you do not overcook the beans so that they stay nice and crunchy.

900g French beans
1 tablespoon vegetable (rapeseed) oil
1 garlic clove, crushed
4 tablespoons sesame seeds

4 tablespoons sesame oil
2 tablespoons reduced-salt
 soy sauce
Dash of Tabasco sauce
Freshly ground black pepper

Serves 4

Put the beans in a pan of boiling water for 3 minutes. Drain.

Heat the oil in a large wok or pan. Add the beans and garlic, fry for 1 minute on a medium–high heat, then add the remaining ingredients. Cook for a further minute and serve.

PER SERVING:
255 KCALS, 21.8G FAT, 2.7G SATURATED FAT, 0.33G SODIUM

broccoli in oyster sauce

This works well with other Asian-style recipes in this book, such as Steamed Sea-bass, Chinese Style (page 110) or Chinese Wok-fried Pork (page 114).

900g broccoli
1 tablespoon vegetable (rapeseed) oil
1 garlic clove, crushed
2 tablespoons oyster sauce

2 tablespoons reduced-salt
 soy sauce
3 tablespoons vegetable stock,
 homemade (see page 138) or
 made with low-salt stock cubes
1 tablespoon sesame oil

Serves 4

Put the broccoli in a pan of boiling water for 2 minutes, drain and set aside. Heat the oil in a pan and add the garlic. Cook for 1 minute on a medium heat then add the broccoli. Add the oyster sauce, soy sauce and vegetable stock. Stir-fry for a further minute, drizzle the sesame soil on top and serve.

PER SERVING:
136 KCALS, 7.5G FAT, 0.6G SATURATED FAT, 0.66G SODIUM

wok-fried tofu and spinach

If anyone says that tofu is boring, tell them to give this one a go. Great as a snack or you can add more vegetables for a complete dinner.

2 tablespoons vegetable (rapeseed) oil
700g silken tofu (or any tofu), diced
150g fresh spinach
1 garlic clove, crushed
Juice of 1 lime or lemon
4 tablespoons reduced-salt soy sauce
1 small bird's eye chilli, finely chopped
2.5cm cube fresh ginger, grated
1 lemongrass stalk, peeled and finely chopped
4 tablespoons water
Handful of fresh coriander

Serves 4

Heat the oil in a wok or a large pan.

Add the tofu pieces and fry on a medium heat for 1 minute, then turn and fry for a further minute. Add the spinach, turning the heat down to low. Add the garlic, lime or lemon juice, soy sauce, chilli, ginger and lemongrass and cook for 1 minute.

Add the water and cook for 1 more minute or so, turning all the time.

Serve garnished with fresh coriander.

PER SERVING:
192 KCALS, 13.2G FAT, 1.4G SATURATED FAT, 0.71G SODIUM

egg-fried rice

A great way to enjoy Chinese food without all the MSG! Kids will love this dish too. This is particularly good with Steamed Sea-bass, Chinese Style (see page 110) and Tiger Prawns in Soy Sauce (see page 98).

4 eggs
1 tablespoon vegetable (rapeseed) oil
600g white rice, cooked
150g frozen green peas
3 tablespoons reduced-salt soy sauce
3 tablespoons sesame oil
6 spring onions, finely chopped

Serves 4–6

Crack the eggs into a bowl and whisk for just a few seconds. In a large pan, heat the oil and cook the eggs as if you were scrambling them.

Add the rice to the pan and mix in well, keeping the heat on low to medium.

Add all the remaining ingredients, heat through thoroughly and serve.

PER SERVING:
392 KCALS, 17.4G FAT, 3G SATURATED FAT, 0.56G SODIUM

avocado and tomato towers

A classic combination of flavours, presented in an unusual way. This is a terrific vegetarian option using great ingredients, but make sure they are ripe and fresh.

6 large tomatoes
Freshly ground black pepper
1 small red chilli, finely chopped
3 avocados
1 lemon
6 spring onions
Handful of fresh basil
1 tablespoon balsamic vinegar
4 tablespoons extra virgin olive oil

Serves 4

Deseed the tomatoes, chop them and season with pepper. Put in a bowl, add the chopped chilli and set aside.

Chop the avocados into small cubes and squeeze the lemon all over them.

Chop the spring onions and the basil finely and add to the avocados. Mix in well.

Place a pastry ring on a serving plate and half fill it with a quarter of the avocado mix. Then top with a quarter of the tomato mix. Lift off the ring and repeat with the remaining mixtures. Drizzle ¼ tablespoon of the balsamic vinegar, followed by 1 tablespoon of the olive oil, all around each of the 4 plates before serving.

PER SERVING:
315 KCALS, 29.9G FAT, 3.8G SATURATED FAT, 0.02G SODIUM

bruschetta with tomato and basil

A wonderful canapé or starter – it is so fresh-tasting and always a winner at any dinner party. Feel free to experiment with your own topping ideas.

I ciabatta loaf, sliced into 2.5cm slices
I large red onion, finely chopped
1 garlic clove, crushed
2 tablespoons extra virgin olive oil
Juice of ½ lemon
1 small red chilli, very finely chopped
Handful of fresh basil
8 medium tomatoes, deseeded and chopped

Serves 4–6

Start by toasting the ciabatta, either under a grill, in the oven or in a toaster.

In a large mixing bowl mix the onion, garlic, olive oil, lemon juice and chilli. Now take the basil leaves, roll them up together, almost like a cigar, and slice. Add these to the bowl, then add the chopped tomatoes.

To serve, top each ciabatta slice with some of the mix.

PER SERVING:
297 KCALS, 9G FAT, 0.8G SATURATED FAT, 0.42G SODIUM

Variation
Bruschetta with pea tapenade This is a nice alternative to the traditional bruschetta topping. It can also be made just as a dip.

Place 200g cooked green peas, 1 crushed garlic clove, 6 tablespoons fromage frais and 2 tablespoons extra virgin olive oil in a blender and whizz until smooth. Spread on the ciabatta and serve.

PER SERVING:
321 KCALS, 11G FAT, 2.1G SATURATED FAT, 0.6G SODIUM

aubergine and feta stacks

This is a very impressive-looking dish – like a creation from a top-class restaurant. It is very simple to make and is always a hit at a dinner party.

2 medium aubergines
3 tablespoons olive oil
10 large tomatoes, deseeded and finely chopped
Handful of fresh basil leaves, shredded
1 clove garlic, crushed

150g feta cheese, crumbled
Freshly ground black pepper
4 tablespoons pine nuts

For the sauce
300g tinned tomatoes
1 small red chilli
1 tablespoon extra virgin olive oil

Serves 4

Preheat the oven to 180°C/350°F/gas mark 4. Slice the aubergines into circles 2.5cm thick and fry in 2 tablespoons oil in a non-stick pan for about 3–4 minutes on each side. Set aside when they are all cooked.

Place the tomatoes in a large mixing bowl together with the basil, garlic and cheese. Now add the remaining oil followed by some black pepper and mix well.

In a non-stick pan with no oil, fry the pine nuts for 1 minute, tossing them continuously so that they do not burn. Add them to the tomato mixture and combine all the ingredients together.

Place 4 of the largest aubergine rounds on a baking tray and drop some of the tomato mixture on to each one. Choose the next biggest rounds of aubergine and place on the top, followed by more tomato mixture, alternating until you have 4 neat pyramid-like stacks. Place in the oven and cook for 10–12 minutes until heated through.

Meanwhile, for the sauce, whizz the tomatoes in a blender with the chilli and olive oil until smooth. Divide the sauce between 4 serving plates, top with an aubergine stack and serve.

PER SERVING:
353 KCALS, 27.1G FAT, 7.1G SATURATED FAT, 0.6G SODIUM

asparagus raft with salmon roe on avocado broth

Avocado is a perfect way to include the right fats in your diet. It is also delicious and this dish is very light and tasty.

24–30 medium asparagus spears
1 ripe avocado
125ml vegetable stock, homemade (see page 138) or made with low-salt stock cubes, cooled
Freshly ground black pepper
60g salmon roe
Herb oil, to garnish

Serves 4

You will need to make the asparagus equal-sized. Taking around 4 at a time and starting at the tips, cut off around 7.5cm. Using one of the 7.5cm tips as a measure, take the same amount off the remaining stalks. Discard the uneven leftovers.

Add the asparagus to a pan of boiling water. Cook for 3 minutes, then run under ice-cold water. This stops the cooking process and keeps the asparagus green and crunchy. Now, in a blender, whizz the avocado and the stock and season well with black pepper.

To serve, put a few spoonfuls of this mix in the base of each plate. Next, make a raft with your asparagus on two levels – the first lined up one way, then the next level going the other way. Top with some salmon roe.

Drizzle some herb oil around the edge of the avocado broth to garnish.

PER SERVING:
121 KCALS, 9.9G FAT, 1.1G SATURATED FAT, 0.23G SODIUM

marinated salmon sashimi

This dish is for the nervous sushi eater – the salmon is marinated in lemon juice which cures the fish, killing any bacteria in the same way that cooking does.

700g skinless salmon
1 medium red onion
Juice of 2 lemons
4 tablespoons reduced-salt soy sauce
1 teaspoon wasabi paste

Serves 4

Cut the salmon into small cubes and set aside in a mixing bowl. Now chop the red onion very, very finely and add to the salmon.

Pour the lemon juice all over the salmon and onion and let it stand for 5 minutes.

In a separate bowl, mix together the soy sauce and the wasabi paste. Add to the salmon and mix well. Refrigerate for at least 30 minutes before serving.

A great way to serve this is in a Martini glass.

PER SERVING:
337 KCALS, 19.4G FAT, 3.9G SATURATED FAT, 0.73G SODIUM

salmon and dill mousse

Salmon is rich in omega-3 oils and low in saturated fat. Don't let the mousse put you off – this dish is quick, easy and foolproof! Serve on salad leaves or with melba or rye toast.

450g skinless salmon
2 tablespoons plain low-fat yogurt
½ small red chilli (deseeded for a less spicy flavour)
Juice of ½ lemon
1 egg
2 tablespoons fresh dill

Serves 4

Put all the ingredients in a blender and blend until smooth.

Divide the mix between 4 ramekin dishes.

Now take a large pan and add water to it, around 2.5–5cm deep. Put the ramekins in the pan, cover and cook on a low to medium heat for 8–12 minutes or until the mousse is firm.

Slip a knife around the edge of each ramekin and the mousse should slide out. Serve cold.

PER SERVING:
226 KCALS, 13.9G FAT, 2.9G SATURATED FAT, 0.07G SODIUM

tray-baked sardines

Sardines are an underrated fish. They are full of all the right oils and so delicious. Drink a glass of rosé wine with this and enjoy – you will think you are in the Mediterranean!

4 lemons
12 fresh large sardines, gutted
2 tablespoons olive oil
2 garlic cloves, crushed
4 tablespoons chopped fresh oregano
Freshly ground black pepper

Serves 4

Preheat the oven to 190°C/375°F/gas mark 5.

Grate the zest from 2 of the lemons and set aside in a small bowl. Squeeze the juice from the zested lemons.

Put the sardines in an ovenproof dish.

In a bowl, mix the olive oil, lemon juice, garlic and oregano. Drizzle this mixture over the fish and season with black pepper. Put in the oven for 25–30 minutes.

Cut the remaining lemons into wedges. Serve the sardines hot, sprinkled with lemon zest and accompanied by the lemon wedges.

PER SERVING:
396 KCALS, 23.8G FAT, 4.4G SATURATED FAT, 0.24G SODIUM

tuna tartare

Make sure that you ask for fresh tuna at the fish counter and say that you will be using it sushi-style. Alternatively, marinate in lemon juice for 20 minutes to cure the fish and kill bacteria (in the same way cooking does).

400g fresh tuna, finely sliced
2 tablespoons chopped spring onions
2 tablespoons sesame seeds
2 tablespoons reduced-salt soy sauce
Juice of 2 limes
2 tablespoons sesame oil
Handful of fresh coriander, chopped
Herb oil, to serve

Serves 4

When slicing the tuna, discard any parts that have a grain as you really want only the flesh you can cut through with ease.

In a bowl, combine the tuna, spring onions, sesame seeds, soy sauce, lime juice and sesame oil. Mix well, then add the coriander.

To serve restaurant-style, take a steel pastry ring around 7.5cm in diameter and place on a serving plate. Fill with the mixture, press down hard and then remove the ring. Drizzle with herb oil. Repeat with the rest of the mixture and serve.

PER SERVING:
255 KCALS, 16.6G FAT, 2.7G SATURATED FAT, 0.37G SODIUM

mediterranean marinated tuna

The tuna in this dish is served raw. If you have any reservations about this you can marinate it in lemon juice for 20 minutes – it will cure the fish and kill any bacteria.

400g fresh tuna, cubed
2 tablespoons sun-dried tomato paste
½ garlic clove, crushed
4 spring onions, finely chopped
2 tablespoons pitted black olives, chopped
2 tablespoons olive oil or vegetable (rapeseed) oil
Handful of fresh basil leaves, shredded
1 tablespoon pine nuts
Juice of I lemon

Serves 4

Put the tuna pieces in a large mixing bowl and add the sun-dried tomato paste, garlic, spring onions, olives, oil, basil and pine nuts. Mix well.

Add the lemon juice just before serving and stir in well.

Press the mixture into metal pastry rings to give it a good shape for serving.

PER SERVING:
240 KCALS, 15.3G FAT, 2.1G SATURATED FAT, 0.12G SODIUM

ken with a honey glaze

This has a superb barbecue taste only without the hassle of having to cook outside. It's a dish that is popular with children. Serve with a salad or baked potato.

3 tablespoons honey
3 tablespoons tomato paste
1 garlic clove, crushed
1 teaspoon white wine vinegar
2 sprigs fresh thyme
1 tablespoon Dijon mustard
4 large chicken fillets, skinless

Serves 4

Preheat the oven to 200°C/400°F/gas mark 6.

Mix all the ingredients together apart from the chicken.

Place the chicken breasts on a baking tray and top each one generously with the sauce. Bake in the oven for 25 minutes and serve.

PER SERVING:
206 KCALS, 2G FAT, 0.5G SATURATED FAT, 0.25G SODIUM

oriental chicken wraps

This dish works equally well with chicken or pork and looks stunning presented in the radicchio leaves. Smaller wraps make great canapés. Serve with warm pitta bread.

1 tablespoon vegetable (rapeseed) oil
1 small onion, finely chopped
10 large mushrooms, finely chopped
450g lean minced chicken
1 garlic clove, crushed
1 tablespoon sesame seeds
1 tablespoon sesame oil
70g tinned water chestnuts, chopped
1 tablespoon reduced-salt soy sauce
1 tablespoon oyster sauce
1 radicchio

Serves 4

Add the oil to a large heated pan and cook the onion and mushrooms for 2–3 minutes.

Add the chicken and garlic and cook for 5–8 minutes, stirring continuously. Once the chicken is cooked add the sesame seeds, sesame oil, water chestnuts, soy sauce and oyster sauce. Stir and cook for a further minute so that the ingredients caramelise and all the flavours blend.

Remove several leaves from the radicchio and fill each one with some of the chicken mix and serve.

PER SERVING:
218 KCALS, 10G FAT, 1.7G SATURATED FAT, 0.41G SODIUM

classic american burger

The best-tasting burger is always made using the finest, leanest beef. This really has to be tried – burgers are rarely made like this any more. Try serving with tomato salsa (see page 135).

1 slice brown bread
1kg lean minced Angus beef
1 garlic clove, crushed
1 teaspoon finely chopped fresh thyme
1 tablespoon tomato paste
1 tablespoon Dijon mustard
1 egg
Freshly ground black pepper
Dash of Tabasco sauce
Splash of vegetable (rapeseed) oil
Toasted sesame-seed burger buns, to serve

Serves 4

Whizz the brown bread in a blender to make crumbs.

Place all the remaining ingredients (except for the oil and the buns) in a large mixing bowl and, adding the breadcrumbs, mix with your hands so it all comes together. Make into patties.

Heat a little oil in a pan and cook the patties for 2–3 minutes on each side; keep on the medium-rare side.

Serve on toasted sesame-seed buns.

PER SERVING:
643 KCALS, 31.8G FAT, 11.7G SATURATED FAT, 0.68G SODIUM

tandoori spiced lamb

This recipe works equally well with chicken or pork. It has great Indian flavours without all the oil. You could cook this on a barbecue outside, if the weather permits!

4 large lean lamb steaks (about 350g in total)
1 lemon, quartered

For the marinade
2 garlic cloves, crushed
1 small onion, quartered
2.5cm cube fresh ginger, grated
2 teaspoons ground cumin
2 teaspoons ground coriander
1 teaspoon garam masala
½ teaspoon cayenne pepper
2 tablespoons lime juice
4 tablespoons plain low-fat yogurt

Serves 4

Put all the ingredients for the marinade in a food-processor and whizz until smooth. Remove any fat from the lamb steaks, then coat them with the marinade. You can keep them marinating in the fridge for a day to develop a more intense flavour, if you have time.

When you are ready to cook the lamb, preheat the oven to 200°C/400°F/gas mark 6.

Put the lamb on a baking tray and cook in the oven for 30 minutes turning twice.

Serve each steak with a wedge of lemon.

PER SERVING:
178 KCALS, 8.2G FAT, 3.5G SATURATED FAT, 0.08G SODIUM

liver and onion on toast

Liver is high in iron and very low in fat. But do note that women considering pregnancy or in the early stages of pregnancy should avoid liver. I love this spread as a starter on toasted triangles.

8 eggs
3 tablespoons vegetable (rapeseed) oil
1 large onion, chopped
450g chicken livers
Salt and freshly ground black pepper
Toasted triangles or crackers, to serve

Serves 4

Start by hard-boiling the eggs (in a pan of boiling water for 5 minutes). Cool, peel and set aside.

Heat 2 tablespoons of the oil in a pan, then add the onion. Cook for around 4 minutes until slightly caramelised.

Add the chicken livers and cook with the remaining oil for about 4 minutes, ensuring that they remain tender on the inside and are not overcooked.

Put the mixture in a food-processor, together with the eggs, and season well. Blend but do not purée – keep it a little chunky.

Serve with toast or crackers.

PER SERVING:
419 KCALS, 22.7G FAT, 4.5G SATURATED FAT, 0.48G SODIUM

4

main courses

penne with sun-dried tomatoes and pine nuts

The way to get the best results with any pasta dish is to add the cooked pasta to the pan of sauce so that it is well coated.

450g penne
100g sun-dried tomatoes in oil, drained
1 small red bird's eye chilli
3 tablespoons extra virgin olive oil
120g pine nuts
1 garlic clove, crushed
Freshly ground black pepper
Handful of fresh basil leaves, shredded

Serves 4–6

Boil the pasta according to the instructions on the packet.

In a blender, whizz the sun-dried tomatoes and chilli until smooth. Add some olive oil if needed but not the oil from the tomatoes as it is too strong.

Heat a large pan and add the pine nuts – toast them without oil, just in the dry pan. This happens quickly, so keep an eye on them and set aside when done.

Now add 1 tablespoon of olive oil to the pan and fry the garlic for 30 seconds. Add the sun-dried tomatoes and remaining olive oil and cook on a low heat for a further minute.

Add the penne and pine nuts. Stir in well, season with black pepper and serve with some shredded basil leaves.

PER SERVING:
723 KCALS, 34.4G FAT, 4.2G SATURATED FAT, 0.39G SODIUM

white truffle and mushroom risotto

It is not only olive oil that is low in saturated fat – try infused oils such as white truffle or sesame oil. They have more flavour and less is required to flavour your cooking.

1 large onion
2 large carrots
6 shiitake mushrooms
6 tablespoons truffle oil
2 garlic cloves, crushed
300g risotto rice
1 glass of white wine (optional)
1 litre vegetable stock, homemade (see page 138)
   or made with low-salt stock cubes
10–14 button mushrooms
2 tablespoons truffle oil and a handful of
   finely chopped parsley, to serve

Serves 4

Chop the onion and carrots finely and cut the mushrooms into thin slices. Set aside.

In a large pan, heat 3 tablespoons of the truffle oil. Add the onion and cook for 2–3 minutes. Add the carrots and garlic and stir for 1 minute. Add the mushrooms and cook for a further minute. Now add the risotto rice and coat with the mix in the pan. Add the wine, if using, and allow to simmer for 1 minute.

Meanwhile, have your stock in a separate pan on the boil. Add it to the rice mixture a ladle at a time and keep stirring for 20 minutes. When you are almost done add the remaining truffle oil.

Divide the risotto between 4 plates, then drizzle some truffle oil around each plate and sprinkle with parsley.

PER SERVING:
538 KCALS, 23.3G FAT, 3.3G SATURATED FAT, 0.15G SODIUM

spaghetti with caramelised vegetables

This can be done with a variety of vegetables, so just use the list below as a guide. Normally Parmesan cheese is added to pasta but you hardly need it in this dish.

450g spaghetti
4 tablespoons extra virgin olive oil or vegetable (rapeseed) oil
1 onion, finely chopped
12 button mushrooms, sliced
12 asparagus spears, cut into 1cm pieces
2 courgettes, diced
1 garlic clove, crushed
1 tablespoon balsamic vinegar
100g sun-dried tomatoes in oil, drained and diced
1 tablespoon tomato paste
Freshly ground black pepper
Handful of fresh basil leaves
Parmesan cheese, grated, to serve (optional)

Serves 4

Cook the spaghetti according to the instructions on the packet. Drain and set aside.

In a large pan, heat half the oil on a high heat, then add the onion and cook for 4 minutes.

Turn the heat to medium and add the mushrooms, asparagus, courgettes and garlic. Add the remaining oil and the vinegar and cook for 5 minutes until all the vegetables are caramelised. Add the tomatoes and tomato paste and stir in well, then add the spaghetti to the pan and coat thoroughly.

Season and add the basil, shredding it as you do so. Serve with a little Parmesan if you wish.

PER SERVING (WITHOUR PARMESAN):
570 KCALS, 17.2G FAT, 2.4G SATURATED FAT, 0.4G SODIUM

gnocchi with wild mushroom sauce

Gnocchi are easy to cook. All you do is add them to boiling water and as soon as they float to the top they are ready. Keep it simple to enjoy the texture.

450g gnocchi
4 tablespoons olive oil
1 garlic clove, crushed
700g mixed mushrooms, sliced
25ml white wine
1 tablespoon white truffle oil (optional)
Chopped fresh chives, to garnish

Serves 4–6

In a large pan of boiling water, cook the gnocchi until they float to the top (this should take around 3 minutes). Drain and set aside.

In another large pan, heat half the olive oil and cook the garlic for 30 seconds. Add the white wine, stir for a few seconds and then add the mushrooms and cook over a medium heat, stirring continuously, for 5 minutes. Add the remaining olive oil and cook for a further 2–3 minutes. Transfer to a blender and blend to a rough texture, not a purée.

Return the mixture to the pan along with the gnocchi and just heat through, coating the gnocchi well.

To serve, drizzle with white truffle oil, if using, and sprinkle with chopped chives.

PER SERVING:
297 KCALS, 12G FAT, 1.8G SATURATED FAT, 0.5G SODIUM

tiger prawns in soy sauce

This dish is really easy to make. Prawns have no fat and should be cooked just until they turn pink – never overcook them. Serve with Egg-fried Rice (see page 79).

25–30 large raw tiger prawns, with heads and shells on
1 tablespoon vegetable (rapeseed) oil
75ml dry white wine
3 garlic cloves, crushed
Juice of 2 large lemons
2 tablespoons reduced-salt soy sauce
6 spring onions, chopped

Serves 4

Start by deveining the prawns. To do this, cut down the centre of each prawn with a knife. If there is a dark vein there, take it out. (This also helps the prawns to absorb all the flavour of the sauce.)

In a large wok (non-stick is best), heat the oil and then add the prawns. Cook for 2 minutes on a high heat, turning frequently. Add the wine and let the alcohol burn off for another minute. The prawns should now be changing colour, from grey to pink.

Add the garlic and cook for 1 more minute, then add the lemon juice and soy sauce. Toss the prawns around and cook until they are completely pink.

Serve garnished with the chopped spring onions.

PER SERVING:
122 KCALS, 3.5G FAT, 0.3G SATURATED FAT, 0.85G SODIUM

mixed bean chilli

A great vegetarian alternative to the traditional meat chilli recipe. Try experimenting with different combinations of beans. The fresh ginger in my recipe adds heat, but you could add chillies as well if you like.

1 tablespoon extra virgin olive oil or vegetable (rapeseed) oil
1 onion, finely chopped
2 garlic cloves, crushed
1 green pepper, deseeded and finely chopped
1 red pepper, deseeded and finely chopped
2.5cm cube fresh ginger, grated
3 tablespoons tomato paste
400g tin chopped tomatoes
400g tin kidney beans, drained
400g tin butter beans, drained
400g tin chickpeas, drained
Fresh parsley or coriander, to serve

Serves 4

In a large pan, heat the oil and add the onion. Cook for a few minutes, then add the garlic. Add the peppers and cook for a few more minutes, adding a little more oil if needed.

Add the ginger, tomato paste and tomatoes. Mix in well for 1 minute before adding all the beans and chickpeas. Simmer for a few minutes so everything is warm.

Serve sprinkled with parsley or coriander.

PER SERVING:
257 KCALS, 5.6G FAT, 0.4G SATURATED FAT, 0.72G SODIUM

salmon fishcakes

These fishcakes are just bursting with flavour. Unlike many other fishcakes these are not deep-fried, making them light and so very fresh. You can adjust the chilli content to your liking.

4 fresh salmon fillets (about 450g in total)
1 red chilli (deseeded if you like it less spicy), roughly chopped
Juice of 1 lime or ½ lemon
1 egg (or enough to bind)
2.5cm cube fresh ginger, grated
1 teaspoon Thai fish sauce (optional)
1 teaspoon reduced-salt soy sauce
2 lemongrass stalks
4 spring onions, sliced
Handful of fresh coriander leaves, chopped
2 tablespoons vegetable (rapeseed) oil

Serves 4

Whizz the salmon, red chilli, lime or lemon juice, egg, ginger, fish sauce (if using) and soy sauce in a blender to a rough consistency.

Peel the lemongrass stalks until you get to the tender root (the point at which you are able to slice through it with ease). Chop roughly and add to the blender. Whizz again for 1 minute.

Stir the spring onions and coriander into the mix.

Mould the salmon mixture into small balls and flatten slightly. Heat a large frying pan and add a drizzle of vegetable oil. Fry the fishcakes, 3 at a time, cooking for 2–3 minutes on each side. Be careful not to move them around the pan until they are ready or they will crumble as there is little fat in the mixture and no bread to bind it. Add a drizzle more oil to the pan as needed. Serve warm.

PER SERVING:
277 KCALS, 19.3G FAT, 3.2G SATURATED FAT, 0.12G SODIUM

poached salmon with five herbs

Another simple dish that makes the most of the flavours of fresh herbs. This recipe works equally well with white fish such as cod or haddock.

4 x 110g salmon fillets, skinless
Handful each fresh:
    basil
    parsley
    tarragon
    chives
    coriander
Freshly ground black pepper

Serves 4

Put the salmon fillets in a large pan. Add just enough water to cover the fish and bring to the boil. As soon as it boils remove from the heat, cover the pan with a lid, and set aside for 15 minutes.

Put all the herbs together and chop until fine. A mezzaluna is perfect for doing this.

Now carefully lift the salmon fillets out of the water and set aside to cool to room temperature, before coating with the herbs on each side. Season with black pepper and serve at room temperature or chilled, with a salad.

PER SERVING:
208 KCALS, 12.5G FAT, 2.5G SATURATED FAT, 0.05G SODIUM

cod baked in couscous and sun-dried tomato paste

If you can't find sun-dried tomato paste, just blend some sun-dried tomatoes with a little olive oil, lemon juice, garlic and basil until smooth.

200g couscous
1 egg
4 fillets cod, skinless
4 tablespoons sun-dried tomato paste
1 lemon
Fresh basil, to serve

Serves 4

Preheat the oven to 180°C/350°F/gas mark 4.

Place the couscous in a bowl. Cover with boiling water and then put a plate on the top. Set aside for 5 minutes. When the couscous is ready, fluff it up with a fork.

Crack the egg into a bowl and whisk for just a few seconds. Now take each cod fillet and dip it in the egg, then coat it with the couscous on all sides. Press down hard to make a crust.

Set all the coated fillets on a baking tray and spread a tablespoon of sun-dried tomato paste on each one using a knife. Place in the oven and bake for 17–20 minutes.

Serve with fresh basil and a salad or mashed potatoes.

PER SERVING:
295 KCALS, 7.8G FAT, 0.7G SATURATED FAT, 0.17G SODIUM

mediterranean-style baked cod

The sun-dried tomato mixture is so easy to make and will last in the refrigerator for many weeks. Use it for other fish and seafood, on bruschetta as a canapé, or with vegetables as a dip.

4 x 175g cod fillets (with or without the skin)
Freshly ground black pepper
6 plum tomatoes, deseeded
1 garlic clove
Juice of 1 lemon
½ small red chilli, deseeded if preferred
1 tablespoon olive oil
Handful of fresh basil leaves
240g tin sun-dried tomatoes in olive oil, drained

Serves 4

Preheat the oven to 180°C/350°F/gas mark 4.

Put the cod fillets on a baking tray and season with black pepper.

In a blender, whizz the plum tomatoes, garlic, lemon juice, chilli, olive oil, basil and sun-dried tomatoes until roughly blended. Spoon some tomato paste onto each cod fillet and bake in the oven for 18 minutes. Serve.

PER SERVING:
264 KCALS, 10G FAT, 1.3G SATURATED FAT, 0.71G SODIUM

whole sea-bass niçoise

All the elements of the Salade Niçoise are here but in this version they are baked in the oven together, and the fish is left whole, giving you maximum flavour.

6 new potatoes, quartered
30 French beans
70ml extra virgin olive oil
70ml lemon juice
4 whole sea-bass, descaled
14–18 pitted black olives
6 anchovy fillets in oil, drained
Freshly ground black pepper
Handful of fresh parsley, roughly chopped, to garnish

Serves 4

Preheat the oven to 220°C/425°F/gas mark 7.

Blanch the potatoes and beans in boiling water for 5 minutes, then drain and set aside.

In a large, deep baking tray, mix together the oil and lemon juice, then put the fish in the tray, side by side.

Put the potatoes on the fish, then scatter the French beans, olives and anchovies all over the top. Season with black pepper and bake in the oven for 40 minutes.

Garnish with fresh parsley and serve with bread – wonderful to mop up all the sauce.

PER SERVING:
418 KCALS, 24.9G FAT, 3.6G SATURATED FAT, 0.54G SODIUM

baked mackerel parcels

You can also cook this on a barbecue, which will make it taste even better. Any white fish can be cooked like this and you can use whichever fresh herbs you have to hand.

2 whole mackerel, gutted and cleaned
Freshly ground black pepper
1 lemon
4 fresh rosemary sprigs
2 garlic cloves, sliced
1 small red onion, thinly sliced
4 tablespoons white wine
Handful of fresh parsley, chopped

Serves 2

Preheat the oven to 200°C/400°F/gas mark 6.

Put each fish on a large piece of tin foil on a baking tray and season inside and out with black pepper.

Slice the lemon, then cut each slice in half. Place the lemon slices inside each fish with a couple of rosemary sprigs and a few garlic slices. Scatter the onion on top and pour the wine over each fish.

Wrap the foil loosely around each fish to make a parcel, and bake in the oven for 25 minutes.

Sprinkle over the chopped parsley to serve.

PER SERVING:
376 KCALS, 24.5G FAT, 4.9G SATURATED FAT, 0.1G SODIUM

sea-bass baked in asian parcels

This is light but with a powerful flavour. It fills the room with an incredible aroma. Ice-fish, snapper or halibut are also suitable for this method of cooking.

2 leeks
4 thick fillets of sea-bass
4 spring onions
4 lemongrass stalks
12 new potatoes, cut in half and
   parboiled for 5 minutes

4 large mushrooms, cut in half
1 small red chilli, deseeded
   and finely chopped
1 large carrot, finely shredded
200ml dry white wine
2 tablespoons coconut milk
Juice of 1 lemon
Freshly ground black pepper

Serves 4

Preheat the oven to 160°C/325°F/gas mark 3.

Take 4 x 30cm squares of foil and make each one into the shape of a large bowl. Double each one up with a second sheet of foil. Slice the leeks into small strings and divide between the 4 foil parcels, placing them in the bottom of each one.

Add a whole spring onion to each parcel, followed by a lemongrass stalk which should be cut in half. Now add 6 potato halves, 2 mushroom halves and a little of the chopped chilli to each parcel. Place some shredded carrot in each one, then place the fish fillets on the top. (Cooked in this way, the fish will steam rather than poach.)

In a bowl, mix the white wine, coconut milk and lemon juice and season with black pepper. Pour over the sea bass in the 4 parcels. Take 4 more large squares of foil and cover each parcel, making it dome-like and folding the joins well so that they are airtight. Now cook in the oven for 40 minutes.

When they are ready, place each parcel on a plate and take to the table. Then, using a large knife, make an incision from top to bottom. This dish is eaten in the foil, which keeps all the flavours and aromas right in front of you as you eat.

PER SERVING:
336 KCALS, 7.2G FAT, 2G SATURATED FAT, 0.17G SODIUM

seared tuna steak and asparagus

The key to cooking fresh tuna is to pan-fry it, searing it on a high heat. This locks in the juices without drying out the fish. Tuna is always better slightly undercooked.

2 tablespoons vegetable (rapeseed) oil or olive oil
4 large tuna steaks
900g asparagus spears
25ml dry white wine
Juice and grated zest of 1 lemon
Handful of fresh parsley, roughly chopped
Freshly ground black pepper

Serves 4

Run the oil over both sides of the tuna steaks. You oil the fish in this recipe, not the pan – it is a great way to cut down on oil without the food sticking.

Break the ends off the asparagus (they will break off at different points, but this is the natural way to remove the hard, inedible parts). Put the trimmed asparagus in a pan of boiling water and cook for 2–3 minutes, then rinse immediately under cold water, drain and set aside.

In a non-stick pan on a high heat, sear the tuna steaks for just 1 minute on each side. Remove from the pan and set aside.

Using the same pan, fry the asparagus on a medium–high heat for 3–4 minutes. Add the wine to deglaze the pan, then add the lemon juice, zest and black pepper to taste and cook for 1 minute.

Transfer the asparagus to a serving plate, top with the tuna steaks, pour the pan juices over the top and garnish with parsley.

PER SERVING:
369 KCALS, 15.8G FAT, 2.7G SATURATED FAT, 0.1G SODIUM

red snapper with orange, lemon and lime

If you have ever been to the Caribbean or the Florida Keys, this will remind you of your visit; it is just so fresh in taste.

Grated zest of 1 orange and 6 tablespoons fresh orange juice
Grated zest and juice of 1 lemon
Juice of 1 lime
5 tablespoons white wine
1 garlic clove, crushed
2.5cm cube fresh ginger, grated
Freshly ground black pepper
4 fillets red snapper
Lemon or orange wedges, to serve

Serves 4

Preheat the oven to 180°C/350°F/gas mark 4.

Mix together all of the ingredients apart from the fish and the citrus fruit wedges.

Make 3 slices on each side of each fish fillet. Now place the fillets in the mixture and refrigerate for at least 30 minutes.

Transfer the fish, together with the sauce, to an ovenproof dish. Bake in the oven for 18–20 minutes and serve with lemon or orange wedges.

PER SERVING:
187 KCALS, 2.4G FAT, 0.4G SATURATED FAT, 0.14G SODIUM

fish risotto

Any fish will work with this recipe. Sometimes your fishmonger or fresh-fish counter may have leftover trimmings – you can get a great mix at incredible value this way.

3–4 tablespoons olive oil
1 large onion, finely chopped
2 garlic cloves, crushed
300g risotto rice
100ml white wine
1 litre fish stock, homemade (see page 139)
   or made with low-salt stock cubes
150g cod, cubed
150g salmon, cubed
150g snapper, cubed
Fresh parsley, to garnish

Serves 4–6

Heat 3 tablespoons of the olive oil in a large pan. Add the onion and cook on a high heat for 2–3 minutes. Add the garlic and stir for 1 minute.

Add the rice and coat with the oil in the pan for 1–2 minutes, then add the wine and simmer for a further minute.

Have your stock ready in a separate pan on the boil. Add it a ladle at a time to the rice mixture, stirring continuously for 20 minutes.

Just 5 minutes before the rice is ready add all the fish and cook through. This takes very little time.

Serve the risotto topped with parsley. I like to use a pastry ring as a mould to make the risotto into a nice, round shape.

PER SERVING:
546 KCALS, 14.4G FAT, 2.3G SATURATED FAT, 0.22G SODIUM

soupe de poisson

This is a classic French dish. The French often serve it with a rouille – a mayonnaise – but I feel there is so much flavour that this is not needed. Serve with crusty French bread.

3 tablespoons olive oil
1 onion, finely chopped
4 garlic cloves, crushed
1.3kg trimmings from 4 medium fish, such as snapper, salmon,
   sea-bass (a mix is great)
3–4 tablespoons tomato purée (4 for a richer taste)
Handful of fresh parsley, chopped
1 bay leaf
Sprig of fresh thyme
Salt and freshly ground black pepper
2 small red chillies, very finely diced
1 tablespoon paprika
1 litre water

Serves 4–6

In a large pan, heat the olive oil and fry the onion for 2 minutes.

Add the garlic and cook for a further minute.

Add all the remaining ingredients to the pan and cook for 1 hour on a low heat. Discard the bay leaf and sprig of thyme before serving.

PER SERVING:
478 KCALS, 21.5G FAT, 3.7G SATURATED FAT, 0.38G SODIUM

fresh fish burger
on ciabatta

If you use fresh fish and grill it, it's as good as any deep-fried fish that I have ever had. The capers and Dijon mustard give this a real kick.

1 tablespoon capers
2 tablespoons light mayonnaise
1 tablespoon Dijon mustard
4 fillets swordfish or halibut, skinless
2 tablespoons extra virgin olive oil
Grated zest of 1 lemon
4 ciabatta buns, toasted

Serves 4

Preheat the grill.

Roughly chop the capers and place in a mixing bowl with the mayonnaise and the mustard. Mix well and set aside.

Place the fish fillets on a baking tray, brush with the olive oil and the lemon zest and grill for 3 minutes on each side.

Top the ciabatta with the mayonnaise mix, then the fish and serve with fresh salad leaves.

PER SERVING:
387 KCALS, 16.9G FAT, 2.7G SATURATED FAT, 0.8G SODIUM

steamed sea-bass,
chinese style

This dish is wonderful in its simplicity – try it with any whole fish. I recommend investing in a steamer: it's such an easy and healthy way to cook fish and vegetables.

4 whole sea-bass (or any whole fish)
4 spring onions, each sliced into 3–4 pieces
2 tablespoons reduced-salt soy sauce
2.5cm cube fresh ginger, grated
2 tablespoons sesame oil
2 tablespoons vegetable (rapeseed) oil

Serves 4

You can either get your fishmonger to remove the scales and gut the fish or you can do it yourself – it is very easy. Just use the back of a knife and scrape up and down the fish. All the scales come off this way. Then slice through the belly and remove everything under cold water to gut the fish.

Place the fish in a large steamer (bamboo is best). Top the fish with the spring onions, soy sauce, ginger and sesame oil and steam on a medium heat for 18–22 minutes.

In a small pan, heat the vegetable oil. Pour the hot oil over the fish to make a crackle on the skin.

Serve with rice.

PER SERVING:
305 KCALS, 16G FAT, 2.1G SATURATED FAT, 0.46G SODIUM

sticky lemon chicken

Taking the skin off the chicken will dramatically reduce the amount of saturated fat without losing the flavour. Serve on a bed of rocket leaves for colour and taste and/or with rice.

8 chicken portions (breasts and legs or thighs)
3 lemons
2 tablespoons runny honey
3 garlic cloves, unpeeled
1 tablespoon extra virgin olive oil
2–3 sprigs of fresh rosemary

Serves 4

Preheat the oven to 180°C/350°F/gas mark 4.

Squeeze the juice from the lemons into a large baking dish. Now add the honey, garlic cloves and olive oil and mix well. Add the chicken pieces to the dish and put the empty lemon halves all around it. (It is surprising how much more juice will be released from the used lemons during the cooking time.)

Put the sprigs of rosemary in the dish and bake for 1 hour. The lemons will come out all sticky and caramelised and can be eaten too.

PER SERVING:
344 KCALS, 17.6G FAT, 4.8G SATURATED FAT, 0.21G SODIUM

italian-style roast chicken

A delicious way to roast a chicken as the stock mixes with the meat juices while cooking, making a sauce inside the bird. Serve with Low-fat Chunky Chips or Roast Potatoes with Sage (see page 76) and some greens, and invite your friends over for a feast!

1 large chicken (corn-fed is best)
4 low-salt stock cubes (chicken or vegetable)
4–6 garlic cloves, halved but unpeeled
2 lemons, quartered
2 sprigs of fresh rosemary

Serves 4–6

Preheat the oven to 220°C/425°F/gas mark 7.

Place the chicken in your sink and rinse through the cavity to clean.

Break each of the stock cubes into 2–4 pieces. Place a few pieces in the cavity of the chicken, followed by a few halves of garlic, then a quarter of a lemon, squeezing it as you push it in. Repeat until all of the cubes, garlic and lemon pieces are inside the chicken. Now slide in the rosemary.

Place in a roasting tin and cover with tinfoil and cook in the oven for 1½ hours, taking off the tinfoil for the last 20 minutes.

PER SERVING:
466 KCALS, 28.7G FAT, 8.2G SATURATED FAT, 0.81G SODIUM

chinese wok-fried pork

Pork can be a very low-fat lean meat. Just make sure that you buy the right cuts. Ask at the meat counter or butcher if you are unsure. This dish can also be made with chicken.

2 tablespoons vegetable (rapeseed) oil
1.1kg lean minced pork
140g tin water chestnuts, drained
1 garlic clove, crushed
12 button mushrooms, cut in half
4 small pak choi, roughly chopped
4 tablespoons water
1 tablespoon oyster sauce
1 tablespoon reduced-salt soy sauce
4 spring onions, chopped
2.5cm cube fresh ginger, finely sliced

Serves 4

Heat the oil in a pan, add the pork and cook for 2–3 minutes, stirring continuously.

Chop the water chestnuts roughly and add to the pan with the garlic, mushrooms and pak choi.

Add the water and then all the remaining ingredients. Cook for 8 minutes.

Serve with rice.

PER SERVING:
465 KCALS, 19.6G FAT, 5.5G SATURATED FAT, 0.61G SODIUM

saffron chicken

Saffron gives food a delicate flavour and incredible colour – a little goes a long way. Serve with some greens for a delicious, stylish chicken dish.

1 large chicken (corn-fed is best)
1 low-salt stock cube
2 lemons
1 onion, quartered
4–6 garlic cloves, halved

3 sprigs of fresh thyme
3 sprigs of fresh rosemary
1 teaspoon saffron
4 potatoes
1 tablespoon olive oil
1 teaspoon paprika
Freshly ground black pepper

Serves 4

Preheat the oven to 220°C/425°F/gas mark 7.

Put the chicken in your sink and rinse through the cavity to clean.

Cut both the stock cube and 1 of the lemons into quarters. Now put them, together with the onion and halved garlic cloves, inside the chicken cavity.

Wedge the thyme and rosemary under the skin above the breast and sprinkle the saffron over the chicken.

Trim the ends of the second lemon and cut it into slices 2.5cm thick. Put these on top of the chicken and in between the legs. This keeps the chicken moist and helps to dissolve the saffron. Cook in the oven for 1½ hours.

Meanwhile, peel and quarter the potatoes and boil in water for 8 minutes. Drain the potatoes and put on a baking tray, adding the oil, paprika and black pepper. Mix well and roast with the chicken for 40–50 minutes, turning once halfway through the cooking time.

PER SERVING:
602 KCALS, 31.4G FAT, 0.4G SATURATED FAT, 0.31G SODIUM

moroccan lamb on couscous

Make sure you use a lean shoulder of lamb for a wonderful flavour and tender meat. If asparagus isn't in season you could serve with roasted vegetables instead.

4 large boneless lamb steaks
258g uncooked couscous
Juice of 1 lemon
4 spring onions, finely chopped
1 tablespoon olive oil
10 large asparagus spears,
    cut into 2.5cm pieces
1 garlic clove, crushed

Serves 4

For the marinade
1 tablespoon reduced-salt
    soy sauce
1 teaspoon honey
Drop of olive oil
1 garlic clove, crushed
4 sprigs of fresh rosemary,
    finely chopped
Juice of 1 lemon

Combine all the marinade ingredients together in a large bowl and add to the lamb steaks. Refrigerate for at least 1 hour so that the flavours are absorbed.

Put the couscous in a bowl and add boiling water to just above the level of the couscous. Cover with a plate to keep in the heat and set aside for 5 minutes. Squeeze over the lemon juice and add the spring onions.

In a large wok, heat the olive oil and fry the asparagus. Add the garlic and fry for 2–3 minutes. Add to the couscous and stir well.

Sear the lamb on a high heat in a frying pan with a drizzle of olive oil. (I do this for 2–3 minutes on each side as I like it rare; for well done cook for 4 minutes on each side.)

To serve, remove the lamb from the pan, slice each steak into 3 pieces and put on a bed of couscous.

PER SERVING:
437 KCALS, 17.1G FAT, 6.6G SATURATED FAT, 0.27G SODIUM

calf's liver wasabi mash

A classic dish that is always a favourite. The key is to never overcook the liver – fry in a pan to lock in the juices and keep it tender on the inside. Serve with some English mustard.

4 large potatoes, quartered
2 teaspoons wasabi paste
4 tablespoons semi-skimmed milk
3 tablespoons vegetable (rapeseed) oil,
    plus a little more for frying the liver
Freshly ground black pepper
2 medium onions, thinly sliced
4 medium slices calf's liver

Serves 4

Place the potatoes in a pan of boiling water and simmer for 20–25 minutes. Drain and mash them with a potato masher or a fork. Mix the wasabi paste with 1 tablespoon of the milk and add to the potatoes. Gradually add the remaining milk and 1 tablespoon of the oil and mash until smooth. Season with black pepper and set aside.

Heat the remaining oil in a large pan. Add the onions and cook for 3–4 minutes. Turn the heat down and cook for a further 3 minutes on a low heat or until the onions are caramelised. Set aside.

Add a drizzle of oil to a frying pan and sear the liver for 2 minutes on each side so that it's nice and pink. (I would even try it for just 1 minute each side to be rare.)

Serve the liver with the mash and top with the onions.

PER SERVING:
389 KCALS, 15.3G FAT, 2.4G SATURATED FAT, 0.11G SODIUM

5

desserts

chilled strawberry soup with fresh mint

An unusual-sounding dish, perhaps, but strawberry soup is a popular recipe with variations all over the world. Try it – it's a wonderful, fresh dessert.

500ml red wine
160g brown sugar
1kg fresh strawberries, hulled
4 tablespoons plain low-fat yogurt
Fresh mint leaves, to garnish

Serves 4–6

Heat the wine together with the sugar in a large pan on a medium heat for 30 minutes until it has reduced and become more of a syrup.

Add the strawberries and cook for a further 2 minutes (or 4 minutes if they are unripe).

Now either refrigerate for serving chilled or serve at room temperature, as you prefer.

Pour some soup and berries into bowls and top with yogurt and mint leaves.

PER SERVING:
287 KCALS, 0.4G FAT, 0.1G SATURATED FAT, 0.04G SODIUM

apricot and orange fool

A perfectly light pudding that is unbelievably easy to make. For those of you who find it hard to make desserts, try this: it's foolproof! Other fruits can be used if you prefer – the choice is yours.

1 tablespoon almonds
150g dried apricots
1 tablespoon honey
2 oranges, peeled
50g plain low-fat yogurt
1 tablespoon brown sugar

Serves 4

Toast the almonds in a dry frying pan until golden (keep a close eye on them as you don't want them to burn). Set aside.

Put all the ingredients except the almonds in a food-processor and whizz until smooth. Transfer to serving bowls and chill in the fridge until needed.

Top with the toasted almonds to serve.

PER SERVING:
151 KCALS, 2.2G FAT, 0.4G SATURATED FAT, 0.04G SODIUM

poached pears with vanilla

Very easy to make and also works really well if you need to prepare ahead of time. The empty vanilla pod can be put into a canister of sugar to make vanilla sugar.

8 small pears
Juice of 1 lemon
4 tablespoons brown sugar
125ml water
750ml white dessert wine
½ vanilla pod, seeds removed

Serves 4

Peel the pears, keeping the stem on them. As soon as you have done this pour the lemon juice all over the pears to prevent them from turning brown.

Put the pears upright in a large pan – you may need to cut the bottoms so that they sit straight.

Add the sugar, water and wine and simmer on a low heat for 10 minutes, then remove the pears from the pan with a slotted spoon. Put them in either one large dish or individual serving dishes.

Add the vanilla seeds to the remaining liquid and stir over the low heat until it is reduced and syrupy. This will take just a few minutes.

Pour the liquid over the pears and serve.

PER SERVING:
226 KCALS, 0.2G FAT, 0G SATURATED FAT, 0.03G SODIUM

grilled fruit

The fruits used in this recipe are very sweet, so only a little brown sugar is needed to caramelise them under the grill. Serve with some plain fromage frais or low-fat yogurt.

2 punnets strawberries
1 punnet blueberries
1 pineapple
2 mangoes
4 tablespoons brown sugar
  (or 6 if the fruit is on the tart side)
1 teaspoon ground cinnamon

Serves 6

Hull the strawberries, slice in half and put in a large bowl. Add the blueberries.

Remove the skin from the pineapple and take out the core. Slice the flesh into 2.5cm wedges and add to the mixing bowl.

Peel the mango and slice into 2.5cm pieces and add to the bowl.

Now add half the sugar and the cinnamon and mix in really well. Transfer to a baking tray and sprinkle the remaining sugar on top. Put under the grill for 3–5 minutes or until caramelised. Serve warm.

PER SERVING:
182 KCALS, 0.6G FAT, 0G SATURATED FAT, 0.01G SODIUM

caramelised oranges

A wonderful Italian-style dish, this is a handy recipe for when you have lots of oranges that need eating up. Cooked in this way, they will keep for a few weeks in the fridge.

8 navel oranges
2 large lemons
300ml water
100g sugar
150ml dry white wine, plus an extra 2½ tablespoons
2½ tablespoons Grand Marnier

Serves 4

Remove the coloured part of orange and lemon zest with a vegetable peeler, cutting from top to bottom to obtain about 1cm x 7.5cm strips. Slice lengthways into very thin juliennes. Set the lemons aside, then trim the tops and bottoms from the oranges, cutting away any pith. You can either keep the oranges whole or slice them. Set aside in a large serving dish.

Bring the water to the boil in a medium saucepan and add the julienned zest, boiling for 5 minutes. Drain in a colander, then transfer to a heavy saucepan.

Add the sugar and the 150ml of wine. Cook on a medium-low heat until the sugar dissolves, then increase the heat to high and boil until the syrup turns a medium caramel colour. Remove from the heat and stir in the liqueur with the 2½ tablespoons of wine.

Pour the syrup over the oranges and serve at room temperature.

PER SERVING:
232 KCALS, 0.3G FAT, 0G SATURATED FAT, 0.02G SODIUM

sesame bananas

An easy and healthy alternative to Chinese toffee bananas, and you don't need many ingredients. This is a really comforting dessert that is popular with children and grown-ups alike!

4 bananas
Juice of 1 lemon
4 tablespoons water
½ vanilla pod, seeds removed
110g brown sugar
2–3 tablespoons sesame seeds, toasted in a dry frying pan

Serves 4–6

Cut the bananas into 2.5cm slices, put in a bowl and squeeze over the lemon juice (this will help the bananas to keep their colour). Set aside.

In a pan, bring the water, vanilla seeds and sugar to the boil. Let it boil until it reduces to a thick liquid.

Now quickly (so that it doesn't harden) drizzle the mixture all over the banana pieces.

Sprinkle over the sesame seeds and serve.

PER SERVING:
246 KCALS, 3.8G FAT, 0.6G SATURATED FAT, 0.01G SODIUM

nmer puddings

A nearly fat-free version of a classic English summer dish that is full of flavour. I like to do the puddings in individual moulds as below, but you could use one big mould if you prefer.

1 punnet each strawberries, blueberries and redcurrants
400g mixed frozen berries, defrosted
50g icing sugar, plus extra for dusting
6 slices white bread, crusts removed
Handful of fresh mint leaves

Serves 4

Hull the strawberries, cut each into 4 and add to three-quarters of the mixed frozen fruit. Add half of the sugar and set aside.

Put the rest of the frozen fruit in a blender together with the remaining sugar and whizz to a purée.

Line 4 ramekins or small pudding moulds with clingfilm. Now cut small circles of bread to form the pudding bases, slices for the sides and larger circles for the tops. Dip the pieces of bread in the purée and use to line the moulds.

Fill the centres with the strawberry and frozen fruit mixture and a little of the purée and press down well, topping with the larger circles of bread.

Place the puddings in the fridge to chill for 30 minutes.

Remove the puddings from the moulds and put on to plates. Pour over the remaining purée and serve with a dusting of icing sugar and fresh mint leaves.

PER SERVING:
216 KCALS, 1.2G FAT, 0.2G SATURATED FAT, 0.23G SODIUM

light crème brûlée

This is a healthy and easy way to make crème brûlée. The traditional method is far more complicated, yet you can still achieve all the flavour this way, without it being too rich.

400g raspberries (strawberries can also be used)
1 teaspoon vanilla essence
300g plain low-fat yogurt
6 tablespoons Greek yogurt
6 tablespoons brown sugar
4 sprigs of fresh mint

Serves 4

Preheat the grill to high.

Divide the fruit between 4 ramekins.

Mix together the vanilla essence and yogurt and pour on top of the fruit in each ramekin.

Now add a thin layer of Greek yogurt to each ramekin to prevent the mixture from curdling.

Sprinkle 1½ tablespoons of brown sugar on each ramekin to cover the surface. Place under the grill for 2–3 minutes until the sugar has caramelised.

Top with a little fresh mint and serve.

PER SERVING:
179 KCALS, 3.1G FAT, 1.8G SATURATED FAT, 0.08G SODIUM

crêpes with asian fruits

A classic French crêpe batter, sweetened with the natural flavours of Asian fruits. These fruits are readily available in major supermarkets; make sure they are nice and ripe.

120g plain flour
280ml semi-skimmed milk
3 large eggs
2 tablespoons brown sugar
Cooking spray or a drizzle of vegetable (rapeseed) oil
To serve
4 tablespoons maple syrup
4 lemons, quartered
1 ripe mango, peeled and diced
6 lychees, peeled and diced
1 ripe papaya, peeled and diced
4 passion fruits

Serves 6–8

Sift the flour into a bowl and make a well in the middle.

Add the milk and eggs and beat until smooth, then add the sugar and beat again.

Heat a non-stick pan (preferably a crêpe pan), using a spray oil if you have one, or a drizzle of vegetable oil if not. Reduce to a medium heat and drop a ladleful of the batter on to the pan. Wait for bubbles to appear (1–2 minutes), then flip. Make more crêpes in the same way until you have used up all the batter.

Drizzle each crêpe with maple syrup and a squeeze of lemon, then add a mix of fruit and roll up. Spoon over some passion fruit seeds and serve.

PER SERVING: 2
42 KCALS, 4.8G FAT, 1.4G SATURATED FAT, 0.07G SODIUM

pumpkin cheesecake

This is a recipe that is a favourite of mine after working in the States. It's easy to make and the cinnamon and pumpkin combination is a marriage made in heaven. A great autumn dessert.

For the base
170g gingernut biscuit crumbs
3 tablespoons brown sugar
2 tablespoons butter, melted

For the filling
700g low-fat cream cheese
170g brown sugar
2 teaspoons ground cinnamon

¼ teaspoon ground nutmeg
¼ teaspoon salt
250g tinned pumpkin (not fresh)
2 eggs and 2 egg whites
2 tablespoons cornflour
2 teaspoons vanilla essence

For the topping
225ml low-fat crème fraîche
1 tablespoon brown sugar
½ teaspoon vanilla essence

Serves 16

Preheat the oven to 200°C/400°F/gas mark 6.

To make the base, mix the gingernut crumbs, sugar and melted butter and press into the bottom of a 22cm springform cake tin. Bake in the oven for 8 minutes, then set aside on a wire rack to cool.

To make the filling, beat the cream cheese, sugar, cinnamon, nutmeg and salt until well blended.

Mix in the pumpkin until combined, then beat in the eggs and egg whites until well blended.

Mix in the cornflour and vanilla essence until blended.

Spoon the cheesecake mixture over the biscuit base and bake for 40–45 minutes or until the centre is almost set. Remove from the oven and cool on a wire rack for 5 minutes.

Meanwhile, to make the topping, combine the crème fraîche, sugar and vanilla and gently spread over the top of the cheesecake. Return to the oven and bake for a further 3–4 minutes until the topping is set.

Remove the cheesecake from the oven and set aside on a wire rack to cool completely. Refrigerate for at least 4 hours before serving.

PER SERVING:
213 KCALS, 8.1G FAT, 4.2G SATURATED FAT, 0.29G SODIUM

raspberry creams

An extremely simple dessert, perfect for a summer's day. These raspberry creams are also a great option if you're looking for a dessert that can be prepared in advance.

300g fresh raspberries
150g low-fat cottage cheese
150g plain low-fat yogurt
3 tablespoons sugar
½ teaspoon vanilla essence
4 sprigs of fresh mint

Serves 4

Put all the ingredients (except for the mint) in a blender and whizz until smooth.

Transfer to ramekins and cover with clingfilm. Refrigerate for at least an hour.

Serve garnished with fresh mint leaves.

PER SERVING:
115 KCALS, 0.9G FAT, 0.2G SATURATED FAT, 0.14G SODIUM

frozen yogurt

I've used raspberries here but any soft fruit will do, and apples and pears work too. If you don't have an ice-cream maker, just put the mixture straight in the freezer. It will have a few crystals in it but will taste just as good.

150g fresh raspberries
200g sugar
600g plain low-fat yogurt

Serves 8

Put the raspberries in a food-processor and whizz to a smooth purée (around 1 minute). Add the sugar and whizz for a further 30 seconds.

Put the raspberry mixture in a medium-size mixing bowl and fold in the yogurt.

Transfer to an ice-cream maker and freeze according to the manufacturer's instructions.

If made in advance, place in the fridge for 30 minutes before serving.

PER SERVING:
143 KCALS, 0.8G FAT, 0.5G SATURATED FAT, 0.06G SODIUM

berry sorbet

Serve this in Martini glasses, garnished with a sprig of mint, either as a course between meals or as a dessert. You can use a mix of berries or just one kind – the choice is yours.

500g fresh berries
Juice and grated zest of 1 large orange
2–3 tablespoons orange liqueur
   (such as Cointreau or Grand Marnier)
175ml water
2 egg whites
100g caster sugar

Serves 6

Put the fruit, orange juice and zest, liqueur and water in a food-processor and whizz until smooth. I like to leave the seeds in but you can sieve your mixture if you prefer.

If you have an ice-cream maker, churn the mixture until it starts to freeze. Alternatively pour the mixture into a rigid container and freeze, stirring every 30 minutes or so until ice crystals start to form and it feels slushy.

Whisk the egg whites until stiff peaks form, then gradually add the sugar, beating until firm and glossy. Fold the meringue mixture into the fruit mixture and continue to freeze and stir until completely frozen. If made in advance, transfer the mixture to the fridge 30 minutes before serving.

PER SERVING:
110 KCALS, 0.3G FAT, 0G SATURATED FAT, 0.02G SODIUM

light chocolate torte

Normally this delicious dessert is made with double cream and lots of butter, but I'm sure you won't feel that any of the flavour or texture has been compromised in this recipe.

Cooking spray or vegetable (rapeseed) oil
240g plain flour
120g unsweetened cocoa powder
240g caster sugar
2 teaspoons bicarbonate of soda
1 teaspoon baking powder
¼ teaspoon salt
½ teaspoon ground cinnamon
275g pitted prunes, puréed
2 teaspoons vanilla essence
2 eggs
225ml skimmed milk
225ml strong coffee
Icing sugar, for dusting
Handful strawberries, to serve (optional)

Serves 14

Preheat the oven to 180°C/350°F/gas mark 4 and spray or grease a 22cm cake tin with oil.

In a large mixing bowl, sift together the flour, cocoa, caster sugar, bicarbonate of soda, baking powder, salt and cinnamon.

Add the prunes, vanilla, eggs and milk and mix well until blended.

Stir the coffee into the mixture, then pour into the prepared cake tin. Bake for 40–45 minutes or until the tip of a knife inserted gently into the centre of the cake comes out clean.

Leave to cool for a few minutes, then sift icing sugar over the top of the torte and serve, with strawberries on the side if liked.

PER SERVING:
204 KCALS, 4.1G FAT, 1.4G SATURATED FAT, 0.31G SODIUM

chocolate fridge cake

Chocolate usually takes a while to cook but this recipe is easy, involves no cooking and is not an exact science like most baking. If you add more or less chocolate it will still work!

125g dark chocolate, 70% cocoa solids, broken into pieces
1 tablespoon golden syrup
125g low-fat spread
125g digestive biscuits, roughly crushed
100g glacé cherries

Serves 6

Line a 450g loaf tin with clingfilm, leaving a little extra over the edge.

Melt the chocolate, syrup and butter in a heatproof bowl over a saucepan of gently simmering water. Stir well, then add the biscuits and cherries.

Pour into the prepared tin. Fold over the clingfilm and put it in the fridge to set – this will take 1–2 hours.

To serve, remove the cake from the tin and slice.

PER SERVING:
339 KCALS, 20.6G FAT, 7.7G SATURATED FAT, 0.27G SODIUM

6

basic recipes

classic french dressing

This is an essential dressing that needs nothing more. It tastes great with French bread as a dip or with any salad. Experiment until you find your favourite extra virgin olive oil.

50ml extra virgin olive oil
25ml white wine vinegar
Juice of 1 lemon
Handful of chopped fresh
  tarragon leaves
Freshly ground black pepper
Pinch of dried herbes de
  Provence
2 tablespoons Dijon mustard

Serves 4–6

Mix all the ingredients together and whisk well until an almost mayonnaise-like consistency is achieved.

PER SERVING:
116 KCALS, 12G FAT, 1.6G SATURATED FAT, 0.22G SODIUM

japanese wasabi dressing

This is a wonderful alternative to an oil-based dressing and is delicious with steamed green vegetables. It's fresh and has a real kick to it. Add as much wasabi as you can handle!

Juice of 1 lemon
1 teaspoon wasabi paste
200g low-fat fromage frais or plain low-fat yogurt
Freshly ground black pepper

Serves 4–6

Mix the lemon juice and wasabi paste together until they are well blended. Add the fromage frais or yogurt and season with black pepper.

PER SERVING:
29 KCALS, 0.1G FAT, 0G SATURATED FAT, 0.03G SODIUM

oriental dressing

This dressing is similar to that used in the Japanese steak houses, and is suitable for drizzling over grilled meat as well as salads. Sesame oil is used here which, like olive oil, is low in saturated fat.

50ml vegetable (rapeseed) oil
50ml sesame oil
Juice of 4 lemons
2 tablespoons reduced-salt soy sauce
2 tablespoons sesame seeds, toasted in a dry frying pan
1 tablespoon wasabi paste
2.5cm cube fresh ginger, grated

Serves 4–6

Mix all the ingredients together well.

Using just a few tablespoons of the dressing per salad serving (a little goes a long way), add to your salad in a mixing bowl and mix well. This is better than pouring the dressing over the leaves on individual serving plates.

PER SERVING:
257 KCALS, 26.5G FAT, 2.9G SATURATED FAT, 0.56G SODIUM

tofu guacamole

This is my take on the classic avocado dip, with tofu added to lighten it. It is an easy way to get more of the super-healthy soya protein into your diet, which is known for its cholesterol-lowering benefits.

3 ripe avocados
Juice of 1 lime
Handful of fresh coriander, chopped

225g soft silken tofu
1 small red bird's eye chilli
4 spring onions, chopped

Serves 4–6

Put all the ingredients except the spring onions into a food-processor and blend to a chunky dip (not a purée). Add the spring onions and mix in well.

Serve with warm pitta bread, crudités or bread sticks.

PER SERVING:
221 KCALS, 20.7G FAT, 2.5G SATURATED FAT, 0.01G SODIUM

thai dipping sauce

This Thai dipping sauce is easy to make and doesn't have any of the preservatives and artificial flavourings found in so many bottled sauces. And, most important, it tastes a million times better.

2 tablespoons caster sugar
Juice of 1 lime
6 tablespoons water

2 tablespoons white wine vinegar
3 red bird's eye chillies, thinly sliced
   (use the seeds)

Serves 2–4

Put all the ingredients in a saucepan and bring to the boil. Cook for 1 minute, then serve with fishcakes, chicken, duck or meat.

PER SERVING:
63 KCALS, 0G FAT, 0G SATURATED FAT, 0G SODIUM

salsa

Salsas are used as dips but they can also work as an alternative to salad dressing, as well as making a superb partner for egg dishes such as omelettes. Spice this recipe up as much as you want by adding more chilli.

8 large plum tomatoes, halved
Freshly ground black pepper
1 red onion, finely chopped
4 spring onions, finely sliced

1 small red bird's eye chilli
Juice of 1 lime
Handful of fresh coriander,
   roughly chopped
1 garlic clove, crushed

Serves 4

Scoop the seeds out of the tomatoes, but do not worry if a few remain. Dice the tomato flesh, put in a bowl and season with black pepper.

Add the red onion to the tomatoes, followed by the spring onions. Mix well.

Chop the chilli as finely as possible and add to the mixture, along with the lime juice, coriander and garlic.

PER SERVING:
55 KCALS, 0.8G FAT, 0.1G SATURATED FAT, 0.02G SODIUM

low-fat hummus

If you're looking for a lower-fat hummus, try this recipe. It tastes great, even without the tahini. Serve as a dip with warm pitta bread and crudités or just spread it on toast as a snack.

450g tin chickpeas
1 garlic clove
3 tablespoons plain low-fat yogurt or fromage frais
Juice of 1 lemon
Freshly ground black pepper
Drizzle of extra virgin olive oil (optional)

Serves 4

Empty the chickpeas into a sieve and rinse through, then drain.

Put all the ingredients, except for the olive oil, in a blender and mix to a smooth paste.

Add a little oil on top of the finished dish to taste if desired.

PER SERVING:
86 KCALS, 2.1G FAT, 0.1G SATURATED FAT, 0.16G SODIUM

tzatziki

A classic Greek dip. Usually this has raw garlic in it, but my version uses roasted garlic, making it less pungent. This is ideal for dipping raw vegetables such as carrots, cucumber and peppers into.

1 garlic bulb
Extra virgin olive oil
1 medium cucumber
200g plain low-fat yogurt
Handful of fresh mint, shredded
200g low-fat fromage frais
Juice of 1 large lemon

Serves 4–6

Preheat the oven to 180°C/350°F/gas mark 4.

Slice through the middle of the garlic bulb and drizzle with olive oil. Push the two halves back together and wrap in foil. Put in the oven and cook for 30 minutes.

Meanwhile, slice the cucumber in half lengthways, scoop out the seeds and discard. Cut the cucumber into thin strips and put in a mixing bowl.

In a separate bowl, put the yogurt, mint, fromage frais and lemon juice and mix together well.

Remove the garlic from the oven and mix 4 cloves into the yogurt mixture. (The rest of the garlic can be kept in the fridge, wrapped in foil.) Add to the cucumber and mix well.

Serve with crudités or pitta bread.

PER SERVING:
69 KCALS, 1.4G FAT, 0.5G SATURATED FAT, 0.06G SODIUM

aubergine dip

This is perfect to serve with crudités or pitta bread. Normally aubergines are cooked with lots of oil as they absorb it all, but this is a great way to cook them without all that fat.

1 large aubergine
2 tablespoons extra virgin olive oil, plus a little extra for brushing
Freshly ground black pepper
2 garlic cloves
3 tablespoons balsamic vinegar
Handful of fresh parsley, finely chopped

Serves 6 as a starter

Preheat the oven to 190°C/375°F/gas mark 5.

Cut the aubergine in half lengthways, brush with olive oil and season with black pepper. Put in the oven and cook for 35 minutes.

Remove the aubergine from the oven and, using a spoon, scoop out all the flesh. Put in a blender with the olive oil, garlic and vinegar and whizz to a chunky texture.

Stir in the parsley and serve.

PER SERVING:
54 KCALS, 4.5G FAT, 0.6G SATURATED FAT, 0G SODIUM

tomato and feta dip

This is an easy dish to make and great to serve for friends with plenty of crusty French bread for mopping. I also use the leftovers as a pasta sauce – in fact it's a good idea to make extra for this reason!

5 tablespoons olive oil or vegetable (rapeseed) oil
600g cherry tomatoes
1 garlic clove, crushed
200g feta cheese
Freshly ground black pepper
Large handful of fresh basil leaves

Serves 4–6

Put the oil and cherry tomatoes in a large frying pan and heat on a medium heat.

After a few minutes add the garlic to the pan.

Cut the feta cheese into 5mm cubes and add to the pan.

Season with pepper (not salt as the feta cheese has a salty taste). Continue to heat until it all just starts to blend and the cheese begins to melt.

Remove from the heat and transfer to a large serving bowl. Slice the basil and add to the dish before serving.

PER SERVING:
278 KCALS, 24.5G FAT, 8.2G SATURATED FAT, 0.74G SODIUM

olive tapenade

There are so many ways to use this – on top of fish before you cook it, on top of bread or served as a dip with crudités. It will keep well in the fridge for a few weeks.

1 tablespoon Dijon mustard
Handful of fresh basil leaves
1 garlic clove
Juice of ½ lemon
1 tablespoon capers
2 tablespoons extra virgin olive oil
425g tin pitted black olives, drained

Serves 4–6

Put all the ingredients in a food-processor and whizz to a chunky mix.

PER SERVING:
154 KCALS, 16.4G FAT, 2G SATURATED FAT, 0.57G SODIUM

vegetable stock

Making your own stock need not be a chore. This is a simple way to make it and you'll see for yourself the difference in the taste alone. Fresh is always best.

2 carrots, chopped
2 onions, quartered
2 celery sticks, roughly chopped
½ fennel bulb, roughly chopped
Stalk from a head of broccoli, roughly chopped
4 large tomatoes
8 button mushrooms, halved
6 black peppercorns
1 dried bay leaf
4 tablespoons tomato paste
3 fresh parsley stalks

Makes 600ml

Place all the ingredients in a large saucepan, cover with water and simmer for 50 minutes.

Strain and use the stock for soups, risottos and more. You can purée the remaining ingredients (minus the bay leaf) for an alternative soup.

PER 100ML:
18 KCALS, 0.1G FAT, 0G SATURATED FAT, 0.05G SODIUM

fish stock

This stock is not hard to make. Always use celery, carrot and onions as staples and you will not go wrong, then you can try being creative by adding your own choice of herbs and spices.

6 large tiger prawns
Heads, skin and bones of 4 fish (sea-bass, salmon, trout, or any fish of that size will do)
OR
4 whole trout, cut into 4 pieces each (a more economical option)
2 carrots, chopped
2 onions, quartered
2 celery sticks, roughly chopped
3 garlic cloves, halved
4 large tomatoes
4 tablespoons tomato paste
3 fresh parsley stalks

Makes 600ml

Put all the ingredients in a large saucepan, cover with water and simmer for 50 minutes. Strain and use as required.

You can put the remaining ingredients (except the heads and bones!) in a blender with 150ml of the stock to make an instant fish soup.

PER 100ML:
22 KCALS, 0.2G FAT, 0G SATURATED FAT, 0.06G SODIUM

chicken stock

The key to a good chicken stock is to refrigerate it, then skim off the fat from the surface. This also makes it much more healthy. Homemade stocks can be stored in the fridge for a few days and also freeze well.

1 chicken, cut into 8 pieces
6 button mushrooms
Scant teaspoon salt
1 teaspoon black peppercorns
2 carrots, chopped
2 onions, chopped
2 celery sticks, roughly chopped
3 garlic cloves, halved
4 large tomatoes
3 fresh parsley stalks

Makes 600ml

Put all the ingredients in a large saucepan, cover with water and simmer for 50 minutes.

Strain, leave to cool and then refrigerate. After an hour remove the layer of fat from the top, using a large metal spoon, then reheat the stock and use as required.

Add noodles for a great chicken soup and save the vegetables from the stock to serve with it.

PER 100ML:
17 KCALS, 0.2G FAT, 0G SATURATED FAT, 0.27G SODIUM

index

UK

H E A R T UK
7 North Road
Maidenhead
Berkshire
SL6 1PE
01628 628 638
www.heartuk.org.uk

British Heart Foundation
14 Fitzhardinge Street
London
W1H 6DH
020 7935 0185
Heart information line:
08450 708 070 (Mon-Fri, 9-5)
www.bhf.org.uk

British Dietetic Association
Charles House, Great Charles Street
Queensway, Birmingham
West Midlands B3 3HT
0121 200 8080
www.bda.uk.com

US

American Heart Association
National Center
7272 Greenville Avenue
Dallas
TX 75231
1-800-AHA-USA-1 (1-800-242-8721)
www.americanheart.org

CANADA

Heart and Stroke Foundation of Canada
1825 Park Road S.E.
Calgary
Alberta T2G 3Y6
(403) 264 5549
www.heartandstroke.ca

AUSTRALIA

National Heart Foundation of Australia
Cnr Denison St & Geils Court
Deakin
ACT 2600
1300 36 27 87
www.heartfoundation.com.au

Heart Support Australia
PO Box 266
Mawson
ACT 2607
0262 852357
www.heartnet.org.au

This revised edition published in Great Britain 2009 by
Kyle Cathie Limited
23 Howland Street
London W1T 4AY
general.enquiries@kyle-cathie.com
www.kylecathie.com

First published 2007 by Kyle Cathie Limited

10 9 8 7 6 5 4 3

ISBN 978 1 85626 867 7

Project editor Jennifer Wheatley
Designer Carl Hodson
Photographer Liz Parsons
Home economist Lorna Brash
Styling Penny Markham
Copyeditor Anne Newman
Editorial assistant Vicki Murrell
Recipe analysis Dr Wendy Doyle
Production Sha Huxtable and Alice Holloway

A Cataloguing In Publication record for this title is available from the British Library.

Colour reproduction by Colourscan